OTHER TITLES BY KEMILA ZSANGE

Past Life Regression: A Manual for Hypnotherapists to Conduct Effective Past Life Regression Sessions

Available at:

www.kemilahypnosis.com/online-store

 Kemilahypnosis   @kemilahypnosis

KEMILA ZSANGE

CAROL'S LIVES

Two Souls' Journey in Two Cities and Beyond

JOURNEY BEYOND PRODUCTIONS

JOURNEY BEYOND PRODUCTION EDITION, 2020

All rights reserved. No part of this publication may be reproduced, stored in a retrieval system, or transmitted, in any form or by any means, electronic, mechanical, photocopying, recording or otherwise, without the prior permission of the author.

Published by Journey Beyond Production.

Library and Archives Canada Cataloguing in Publication

Zsange, Kemila, author
Carol's Lives / Kemila Zsange.

ISBN: 978-1-7775089-0-6

Cover design: Silmara Emde, The Orange Lamp House

First Canadian Edition: December 2020
First International Edition: December 2020

To

Carol Jane Benjamin

and

Richard Adam Miller ~

We have never met you in person, perhaps because we are closer to you.

Contents

Preface 1
1 Let's Have a Past Life Discovery 9
2 Blanket Speaks 19
3 Black High Heels, Baby! 27
4 The First Time, Once Again 45
5 Chestnut Street 55
6 "Tim, Keep Her" 63
7 "I'd Like Another Drink" 71
8 The One Who Travels 79
9 Ocean Waves, Anciently Young 89
10 Trial Times 99
11 The Rumpelstiltskin 107
12 The Story of Me and My Owner 121
13 Are There Fish in Your Ocean? 125
14 A Spy in the Sky 131
15 Onto the Promised Path 137
16 Like Becoming a Butterfly 151
17 New York, New York 163
18 Shelter from the Storm 171
19 The Fear of Living 185
20 Richard Miller 191

21 It Doesn't End 201
Epilogue 207
Acknowledgements 211

Preface

I started writing this book during a beautiful, white Christmas in 2015 on the Canadian Prairies in Saskatoon, Saskatchewan, with my partner Tim's family. This was roughly four months after I had made the decision to share these stories with you ... Well, kind of decided.

In August of that same year, I had invited Orlea Rollins down from Whitehorse, Yukon to Vancouver, British Columbia. Orlea is a medium intuitive, a psychic and a channeler. We had uncovered her gifts when she and I first started doing Past Life Regression, Life-Between-Lives Regression and Future-Life Progression during our Skype hypnotherapy sessions for her. It had become clearer and clearer to me during this time that Orlea was highly gifted in her intuitive and channeling abilities. Some people say there are clairvoyant, clairsentient, clairaudient, and claircognizant. I found Orlea had all these clair-whatever open. Towards our last sessions, I told Orlea what I had observed and I must have encouraged her to pursue sharing her abilities. I did not remember doing so, but a year or so later, Orlea sent me an email thanking me for supporting her in exploring those gifts. She wrote:

> "... A lot has changed since we spoke last. The biggest change is I have been blessed with hearing my Spirit Guide and Guardian Angel speaking to me telepathically. I am able

to channel for others, and I have you to thank for bringing my attention to this gift that has been bestowed upon me. I recall after one of our sessions that you told me you thought I could be a Channeler. If you had not spoken those words to me, I may not have tapped into this possibility. Nor given it another thought. Of course, I continue to practice and learn something new every day.

I trust this reaches you in good health, joy and with positive energy.

Take care and wishing you a lovely day :)

In light, love, and spirit,
Orlea"

Orlea's email reminded me of my observation of her gifts. It is always my greatest joy and passion to see and help people do what they have intended to do in the life they live; maybe even before they embarked upon this physical lifetime.

Six months after this email I received another one from Orlea:

"… I must tell you that if it were not for you, I would not be a Channeler and able to channel other people's Spirit Guides, Guardian Angels, pets, and loved ones. I cannot thank you enough for awakening my conscious to my Higher Self and re-connecting with my spirituality. You are an amazing and beautiful soul, Kemila. I do hope our paths will connect again. Take care.

In light, love, and spirit,
Orlea"

The email brought a huge smile to my face. I felt very inspired by her taking actions and allowing her gifts to come through this way. So, while packing for a vacation to England and Paris, I wrote Orlea back:

> "... Next time you come to Vancouver, let me know. Maybe I can organize a Psychic Reading Circle for you where a group of people get together, and you intuitively read for them, not necessarily in any particular order. I know you have everything that it takes to do things like that. You are a very clear channel who has just about all the senses open - seeing, hearing, and knowing. The only thing that could possibly be in the way would be your confidence. But confidence is something you can simply give to yourself. So, it's a given."

I did not want her to feel any pressure or obligation. So I used the word "maybe" in my email. Again, Orlea proved herself an action-taker on this matter. She wrote, "... Your offer is very generous. And, I am going to take a leap of faith and trust that I am meant to take you up on your offer."

We soon worked out the details and in August 2015, Orlea flew from Yukon to Vancouver for a four-night stay. During her visit, I organized three psychic reading circles for her. The turnout was incredibly good—beyond our expectations. I felt sorry that we had to say no to some people due to the circles being fully booked. I was not sure if the overwhelming response was because this type of information was so greatly needed. Or, because of the invisible, yet palpable, halo that Orlea emanates.

As Orlea stayed with me during her visit to Vancouver, we were able to spend a lot of time together. We talked about how strange it was at the very beginning of our hypnotherapy sessions that I felt an unconscious connection to her. So much so, upon saying good-bye at the end of our first 30-minute Skype consultation, the words "I love you" just slipped out instead. I immediately felt embarrassed and explained it was not my usual manner of saying "Good-bye" with new clients.

We also discussed how Orlea would use these group readings as a stepping-stone towards her unknown future endeavours; how we may be having psychic reading circles in the woods of Stanley Park near my home. I shared my upcoming travel plans with her. And told Orlea how Tim and I had met—how we had found each other in past lives. The conversation very soon led to our favourite past life—as it always did. Maybe because it was my most recent lifetime. Perhaps, it was because we had switched genders in that life. In any case, it did not matter. I am always willing to tell that story to anybody who is ready to listen. Over the years, I had told the story of Tim and I to many of our friends who are open to the metaphysical. To some of them, I have probably told it too many times.

It was that very same August, with Orlea and I gathered around the dining table, facing the windows which overlooked the cedar trees of Stanley Park, that I again began narrating my story to her. Orlea was intrigued. Suddenly a light bulb went on in my head: *To write about it*. At precisely that moment, Orlea declared, "Here's your next book!"

I looked at her, half smiling with my mind running its habitual circuit. "But how?" I said. "The first book was easy. It was a manual. I don't know how to write stories."

Orlea stared at me. And stared at me. And stared at me some more. In all likelihood, she could not believe those words had just come out of my mouth. I was the one who always knew how to motivate and encourage others to do the "impossible".

"Alright," I conceded. "May I mention your name in the book? I think I will know how to write the book if I start writing about our conversations. I trust the rest will always come if I simply start it."

Orlea nodded her head in consent.

The next person I needed permission from was my partner Tim. He did not particularly like the idea of making our story public. Being a person who is scientific and self-identifies as an engineer; Tim has never really known what to make of those stories that came out of his own hypnosis regression sessions. But he could not find a reason that, as far as he knew, would be enough to convince me not to write it. Deep down, we both knew, I was the one who does the persuading. I can't help it. After all, I am the hypnotist in the family.

Tim originally suggested that I write *Carol's Lives* as a work of fiction. I thought about it and agreed. At the time, I thought that non-fiction books implied that everything had to be "real". Even though at least half of the material in this book is from Past Life Regression sessions, there was no way for me to prove the truth of these lives. Nor did I care to get into an argument about how real it was for the individuals having—or is it *living*?—these experiences. So, I settled for the "Fiction" category.

Ironically, while writing *Carol's Lives* as a book of fiction, I felt a sense of freedom staying true to the transcriptions of some of the hypnosis sessions captured here. Especially, for those more "other worldly" stories. Fiction can permit the writer to express concepts, ideas, and story arcs in a clearer and effortlessly creative way. Not unlike the movies and television show *Star Trek*, it is less complex to present non-earthly lives in a fictional way. At the same time, collective thinking of the broader public waits for scientists to catch up, and for governments to announce the existence of galactic life.

However, as I was working on the last few pages of this book, I realized it wouldn't truly come across as a work of fiction to you, the reader. Within the frame of these stories, everything *has* happened. These retellings are far too personal to truly be considered a fictional account. Rather, it is a memoir of specific times, places, people, and events.

Of course, one might argue, "Everything is made up." The truth of my story can only be as accurate as my memory serves and my records show.

So, you will decide for yourself how you want to read my story. As I present to you, my memoir of two soul's journeys in two cities, and beyond.

Kemila Zsange

November 2020, Vancouver, BC

1

Let's Have a Past Life Discovery

I did not know where this was going to lead me, when one day, out of great curiosity and a little trepidation, I asked my nephew Devin to try doing a past life regression session with me. I did not know what to expect. In fact, I was incredibly nervous.

Devin was living with my partner Tim and I, as an international high school student. And I was fresh out of graduating from a two-year clinical counselling hypnotherapy program.

During the program, our instructor had told us that "weight loss" and "quit smoking" was where the money was in this profession, and it would be wise to focus on these areas in our practice. Accordingly, I planned to start my practice treating people's mental, emotional, and behavioural issues.

At some point, I became aware of my growing fascination with the more spiritual aspects of hypnosis. That very same fascination was present when I finally learned that it was possible to access past lives through hypnosis. Even though I had not registered for the Hypnotherapy Program with the intention of doing past life regressions, taking the course helped to place me squarely on that path.

For a long time, I had delayed asking Devin. I had hoped to "exchange" nephews with another newly graduated Hypnotherapist to avoid any embarrassing situations. What if I had killed my nephew, or if he me, in a previous life? After all, didn't they say souls travel together in different lifetimes due to karmic debts? Wasn't humanity's a history of violence? One person or group killing another or vice versa for one reason or another?

But I could not find another Hypnotherapist from my class who was as keen as I about exploring past lives. Most of my classmates likely did not believe in it. Those who did, were significantly discouraged by our instructor's instruction: "We do *not* do Past Life Regression on purpose. When it spontaneously happens, deal with it."

Keen to experiment, I looked around and found my nephew was the only person with whom I could afford to fail in this endeavour. It would not be a big deal for him. At the time, Devin was an easy-going teenager; one immersed in the world of online gaming. He was relaxed about his new life, despite living away from home, in a new school and a new country.

Devin has since grown into a self-confident young man, and most things are still not a big deal for him. My first book *Past Life Regression: A Manual for Hypnotherapists to Conduct Effective Past Life Regression Sessions* was dedicated to him, as he was the one who helped me out when I first started. But as far as I know, my nephew seemed not to care about such sentimentality. He has not, and probably will not read it, even though I told him a book with his name in it is travelling all over the English-speaking world.

It was that relaxed attitude of Devin's at the beginning that enabled me to try and not be concerned about failure. Devin would do it simply because I had asked. He did not question me; he did not seem to need to know what for, how, how long, or how far we would go.

My 18-year-old nephew seated himself comfortably on the club chair in my bedroom and closed his eyes. His eyelids quickly fluttered. After a short while, he found himself in Japan as a 7-year old boy playing with his little sister in the backyard of a nice house.

Oh my God! I could not believe it! So vivid, so real, so true! So easy! I paused, opened the bedroom window, and took in a deep breath of fresh air before I could continue the session.

The little boy in Japan grew up to become a very successful businessman in real estate. In the 1980's when he was in his 60's, he died unmarried and alone. The only person who had been close to him his whole life had been his younger sister, who married and had children.

That past life regression session of Devin's was the start of something incredibly significant in my life. Thanks to my nephew, he made me feel success could be easily attained when undertaking such sessions.

After that first session, Devin and I did a few more past life regressions. It was then that his Soul's theme became clear to me: my dear nephew was always alone and left feeling lonely at the end of a life. Intrigued, I discussed my past life regression discoveries with my partner. I had wanted to have a session with Tim, too. For a while, nothing else mattered more to me. But Tim did not buy into those New-Agey beliefs. A life *before* Tim? No way, not plausible. You have got to be kidding. There was none. A woman's egg and a man's sperm. That was all there was to it, as far as "before Tim" went.

But some of my recounting of Devin's past life regression stories must have resonated with Tim. In hypnotherapy, using targeted key words is a common practice for getting through to a person's subconscious mind. And Tim had been an engineer who loves science to this day. So instead of "regression", I knew that using words like "exploration" and "discovery" would speak to him.

One day during a relaxing bath, I must have been describing something too excitedly to Tim. To my surprise, he uttered, "Cool. I would like to explore that too."

For a moment, I could not believe my ears.
Wow. Great! Really? Oh, I cannot wait!
I managed to keep my excitement in check. Too much enthusiasm sometimes scared him.

"Are you sure?" I had asked. Haltingly I stumbled through thoughts and questions about scheduling a suitable time to do it. Despite my best efforts, my excitement got the better of me. "But … if you really want to explore it … Let me see. Maybe … next … Is Thursday okay? Otherwise we'll have to do it much later. I'm quite busy this week."

"Sure. Thursday works fine."

"All right. I'll put you in my calendar to make sure it's happening then."

Thursday came and found Tim lying on the couch. "What areas would you like to explore?" I softly asked.

"Anything at all would be fine."

"We will free flow then."

"Free flow sounds perfect to me."

I was nervous. I had just graduated from my nephew, an open and carefree youth, to a sceptical and logic-based adult. Even though this was still an unpaid "friends and family" type of session, I felt that there was no room for error with this one. In case anything about our karma came up, I acquiescently suggested to Tim, "If there is anything that you want to keep to yourself, that is all right. Just let me know and we will move on."

It took me a lot longer to get Tim into a deep enough state for past life regression than it had for Devin. Devin was younger with no agenda other than to simply go along for the journey. Tim on the other hand, while generally an open-minded person, also had a lifetime of attitudes and beliefs to contend with.

First, I had Tim focus on my pen which I held in front of him above his eye level, and I slowly began the hypnotic induction. "Give yourself permission to go into hypnosis. Nod your head without moving your gaze if you are ready … Your eyelids are getting heavier … and they will blink." I timed my words to the movements of his eyelids. "Allow your eyes to gently close and remain closed on one of your exhales."

Once Tim's eyes were fully closed, I followed up with a progressive relaxation technique. Progressive Relaxation is a common practice which supports a person in becoming more deeply relaxed. Starting at one end of the body, I bring their awareness to one set of muscles and guide them to relax those. I then shift their focus to the next set of muscles as we systematically work our way through their body. Tim was completely relaxed by the time we finished. So, I closed the induction with a simple deepening, instructing him to visualize taking an escalator downward.

Tim's first regression into past lives turned out to be a primitive life. He was living in an icy cave-like structure and was male with a wife. There was a fire in the centre of the structure to keep out the cold. Everything was simple in that life, including the story itself. After a short time, his wife died. Caveman Tim ended up living the rest of his days feeling very lonely. Towards the end of Tim's session, there were two streams of tears silently running down his face.

I wondered about the theme of loneliness that ran through those past life regression sessions of both my nephew and my partner. I don't know what their thoughts were about their past lives. But I was comforted by holding onto the thought, that at least they had me in this life. In that moment, I made up my mind to love them as much as I could, for as long as I could.

Thrilled as I was with the "success" of facilitating a past life regression with a second person, I did not know what to make of the session with Tim. For the longest time, emotions from both my professional and personal lives became intertwined. My delight, however, with this success was magnified by the fact that during my Counselling-Hypnotherapy training, we had not been taught *how* to do Past Life Regression sessions. The instructor held his own religious beliefs. As unbiased as he tried to be, he did not seem to want to get into this "grey" area in his teaching. He informed us that one way to explain what comes up in a "past life regression" was that it is genetic. That is, we each carry the genetic profile of our ancestors all the way back to the beginning of time. So, the "past life regression" experience could be described as a genetic "memory". Even though my instructor never denied reincarnation theory, he simply chose not to emphasize it in the curriculum he presented to us. During the entire two years of the program, we had watched one video on Past Life Regression, and five slide shows on this topic. That was it. I must have been doing past life regression sessions in another life. I really cannot find another explanation for my fascination, enthusiasm, and proclivity for it.

If Orlea is a client-turned-friend, I also have quite a few friends-turned-clients. One such client once said, "I don't understand why so many people are interested in sports shows. More people should be more interested in past life regressions. Because, in a sports game it is always certain one team will win, and one will lose. But with this past life regression stuff, you never know what's coming up. It is to find out more about me, ourselves. Everyone should do it, multiple times. A session is not even more expensive than a game ticket!"

At the time, I could not agree with her more. My client's comment helped me delightedly visualize a stadium-full of people flowing into my practice for past life regression sessions. But today, years later, I would not agree with that. Why would *everyone* be interested in using past life regression to find out more about themselves? We can discover and explore our unique selves through anything, including sports shows. In everything we do, there is an opportunity to learn more about ourselves. People can choose to learn in the manner best suited to them, that resonates with them the most. Exploration of past lives through hypnosis is simply one such tool on the path of self-discovery.

Now that the door to one past life had opened for Tim, I wondered whether he would agree to another session with me. I hoped the tears of sadness would not turn him off from further exploring his other lives, but instead, make him more curious. Tim could easily explain it all away by claiming it had been his overly active imagination. But how would he account for the tears?

I was still not certain. If it were me, I would be interested in unpacking those emotions. But Tim was not me, and I could not speak for him. Some people are more scared by, than curious about, their unconscious feelings. And often, when I thought I understood Tim, I would be quite wrong. Even on things we agreed upon, if we delved deeper, we would discover that we each used a hugely different thought process to get to that same place. We are now both aware of how extreme our differences in thinking and reasoning can be. So much so, that you would wonder why or how we came together in the first place. Well, it was not exactly "love at first sight". Emotionally speaking, it was completely drama-less when we first met. But that does not mean there wasn't a story. In fact, it was quite a story.

2

Blanket Speaks

Sunday, July 1, 2007. Canada Day. It was a gloriously beautiful sunny day.

Vancouver has been dubbed Rain City. On average, there are 166 days per year of rain. That is almost half the year. Even in the summertime, it is not always dry. This city is a shape shifter. When it rains and when it shines, I feel as though I am in two completely different cities. It knows how to transform itself from one way to the other.

I had heard there was a Jazz Festival going on with some free concerts in and around the Roundhouse Community Centre. Spending my first summer ever in Canada, I could not and would not, find a better thing to do on that bright and beautiful day. So, I headed toward the Roundhouse with the science fiction book *Variable Star*, co-authored by Robert Heinlein and local Vancouver writer Spider Robinson, neatly stowed away in my bag.

A funktronica styled band was playing on the sizable stage that had been erected near the entrance of David Lam Park near the Roundhouse. The park was surrounded by vendors selling typical festival goods. I walked from one side of the stage to the other, browsing through all the booths and stalls. Tonnes of people had brought lawn chairs and blankets from home to sit or lie down on and enjoy the free show. I had brought nothing of the sort with me.

The band finished. The emcee was announcing the next show, which was due in about 40 minutes. People in the crowd started to get up and move around. But I was ready to sit down after all my Canada Day window shopping. *Wouldn't it be nice if I had a blanket like those lying there, so that I could sit and enjoy the sun with my book?* As if through magic, to my right I spotted an unoccupied, big, light purple and white checked blanket lain out on the grass. It looked so inviting; lovely and lonely, just waiting for me to take my seat on it in the sun. I found it hard to resist its pull. But I was resisting.

No. This must be someone else's blanket.

But nobody is there now. And my feet are tired. I need to sit on something just like that.

You don't really want to steal a blanket, do you?

If I don't take it away, it's not stealing. It's borrowing.

But how can you call it borrowing without the owner's permission?

Maybe the owner has already abandoned the blanket. Maybe someone just didn't bother to take it back home after that last act.

What if the owners just left for a while and they will come back? That would be really embarrassing.

If they come back ... then ... maybe, I will make a friend or two!

Strangely, the prospect of making new friends excited me more than sitting on the blanket itself. To date, I had not made friends with strangers in Canada easily. Or, so I thought. I still cannot explain why the idea of making new friends thrilled me so much that sunny Canada Day in David Lam Park.

Later, I had explained many times to Tim that it was not in my nature to take other people's things without first seeking permission. Nor, was it my nature to look forward to making friends with people I did not even know existed, but that day had been different. That sensation of being called by that comfy, faded blanket is unmistakably clear to this day. Somehow, following that feeling made more sense than resisting it. However strong the rationale for not doing so was.

It was a good-sized blanket, about five feet by seven. I accepted its warm invitation, sat down, took out my book, and began to read. Peripherally, I was paying attention to people's feet coming and going around me. Occasionally, I would even look up nervously, or expectantly, only to feel relieved when I saw them walking away in another direction. Half an hour passed. I got more comfortable sitting there and decided not to care about the foot traffic around me anymore. I started to wonder if anyone was going to come back to the blanket at all.

Canadians are very rich and generous! They come out to a park, lay down a blanket, enjoy the music, and then they leave the blanket behind. This is a well-used blanket, but it is still nice and functional. Hand crocheted. It is pretty. At the end of today, if still nobody comes to claim it, I am going to take this blanket home with me.

With that thought, I became the proud, new owner of the twice-loved blanket. Another band was starting to play, and more people were gathering back and settling down to listen. A young couple with a much smaller blanket squeezed into a little patch of grass behind me. The woman gradually put her feet onto my bigger blanket. I turned back to glance at her. I didn't intend anything by it. I was just looking.

"Oh! I'm sorry," she said and took her feet off "my" blanket.

"Don't worry about it," I replied and went back to reading my book. I must have done so quite graciously and naturally. It felt funny. It wasn't even my blanket. With the live music playing on stage, I laid down on my back looking up at the infinite blue sky. Turning over on my stomach, I went back to reading. To the rest of world around me, it *was* my blanket. Why would they think otherwise? Especially, when I was so thoroughly enjoying my day in the park on it. But, not to the one who was walking my way in that very moment.

The moment I saw him, I knew it. He wore a short-sleeved, light green and white checked shirt—the fast-dry type of travel shirt—light blue khaki shorts, leather sandals, and carried a big Canon camera with a long lens. He walked from the direction of the front of the stage, still quite far away. But I knew immediately he was walking towards the blanket—*his* blanket. I had just enough time to quickly put my book and water bottle away, stand up, and leave. But I did not move.

He looked warm and kind, the type of person who I could immediately trust. He was in front of me now. As if I were transparent, he just looked at his blanket.

I said sheepishly, "Sorry, I didn't mean to take your blanket. I just didn't see anybody here for quite a while … I … I'm leaving now, though. Thank you."

Still not looking at me, he gestured something like, "No worries."

I had started to pack up my book and water bottle and pull myself up. He sat down on the edge of the blanket, looking intently at the LCD screen on his camera. He must have taken a lot of photos as there were more concerts going on inside the Round House Community Centre.

This is really a big enough blanket for a whole family.

I looked at him again, bent down, "Is it okay if I still sit here on this little corner of the blanket?" Where had I gotten that courage from?! "It's a big enough blanket, and I really like this band."

"Huh? Oh yes. Sure!" That was the first time Tim spoke to me. Then he went back to examining the contents of his camera. I sat back down; this time more properly conducted.

Maybe twenty minutes passed. I felt a little awkward silently sharing the same blanket with a stranger. He was still going through his multitude of photos.

"So, are you a journalist?" I asked.

Afterwards and many times over, we would tell our story of how we met to friends and family alike. Tim would always emphasize that *I* was the one who came up with the opening line.

That was a pretty unique pick-up line. Wouldn't you say, Hon?

He responded, no, he was not a journalist. But funny that I had asked. He had just been invited by a friend of his to make his first documentary film. So, my guess was not that far-fetched after all.

The rest of the conversation was completely organic. We shared stories of our travels. We were pleased to note there were quite a few places in the world that we both had visited. Tim was impressed that I knew the correct positions of the tongue and teeth in order to pronounce English words properly. As a native speaker he certainly never learned English that way. We talked and talked and talked. The conversation went on as if time stood still.

And maybe time did stand still. I was completely unaware that I may have known Tim before. It was like taking a fish out of a pond and putting it into a lake. The fish does not need to register the idea of different sources of water when it is already swimming in it.

While we were talking, I glanced at him, still feeling the warmth and kindness emanating from him. Hours passed us by, and Tim finally remembered to introduce himself, "I'm Tim." We shook hands. Tim mentioned he was going to make a documentary about Buddhism.

"Buddhism!" I was instantaneously interested. "Well, in the country I came from, Buddhism is said to be the dominant religion. But I don't know much about it. I'm very interested in how you'd present it in the documentary." I dug out my business card from where I worked at that time. "You have to let me know when your documentary comes out. I'd be very interested to watch it."

I don't know what would have happened if I had not given Tim my card.

It was the last band of the day. And it was getting dark, yet the music and the crowd had gotten hotter. A band from Mexico was playing a funky fusion of reggae, jazz, and salsa. Everyone around us was standing up and dancing. Tim and I remained seated on the blanket and we continued talking amongst the jungle of moving and grooving limbs.

The day's free show came to an end. I planned to walk north to watch the fireworks at Canada Place on the waterfront, and Tim was heading west to his home. It was a strange unfinished feeling as we parted ways—comfort, excitement, contentment, uncertainty. From behind me, I felt Tim's gaze lingering. I didn't know if he was single, but he did not seem to be interested in knowing if I was either. Much later, Tim would share that he just knew he was going to see me again.

3

Black High Heels, Baby!

It was not until three weeks after Tim's caveman life regression, that I was able to find an opportunity to set up another session with him. My birthday was coming up, and Tim had asked me what I would like to get as my birthday gift.

"Another past life session with me!" I had exclaimed without hesitation.

Tim was predictably surprised. He gave me a strange look. I felt strange, too. Something was not right. I was supposed to be paid to do this. Yet, he had received all these sessions for free. And now, I felt as though he were doing me the big favour by agreeing to a session in the form of a birthday gift.

I so wanted Tim to want it too. But arranging things was not going as smoothly as I had hoped. For me, three weeks was a long time to wait. Take the analogy of a sports lover: many sports fans would go crazy to get a ticket to a game. Personally, I would not care. I often say, that to get me to watch live sports—other than something graceful and artistic like figure skating—not only would I need a free ticket; you'd also have to pay me to go! And just as some people eagerly save up to attend a game, others save up to have one exciting past life regression experience. For Tim, however, I needed to employ key persuasive strategies such as scientific wording, begging, and my birthday wish.

I got the impression that Tim wanted me to want something else for my birthday. But I did not care about anything else. Call me obsessed. I only wanted what I wanted.

To pique genuine interest and make the experience more "exploration worthy" for Tim, I suggested we target on going back to a past life that could be historically verified. I made a note to pose questions about detailed facts, such as geographic locations, years, types of food eaten, and place descriptions. Hopefully, we could then research and verify the facts afterwards to appease his scientific curiosity.

The actual session took place the evening after my birthday. I began by having him use his imagination to gently float up from where his body was. Floating up to the ceiling, he could look down at his body lying comfortably on the couch with me seated on the chair beside him. I then guided him to float out of the window, up higher, to where he could see the rooftop of our home and Stanley Park spread out in front of it. In my measured monotone, I guided Tim's awareness to continue to float up to where he could see more of the city, the park, English Bay, Burrard Inlet, and beyond to the snow-capped North Shore mountains. We continued all the way up, until Tim eventually had an astronaut's view of our green and blue, visibly rotating Earth below him.

After some time-distortion suggestions to shift Tim's ability to track the passage of time and affect his perception of it, I slowly had him float back to the Earth. "When I count from 20 to 1, you will slowly come back … landing on the Earth … in another time … in another place … in another body … living another life you have lived … about which you will be able to research later."

I then counted slowly from 20 to 1, bringing him back down to Earth. "… 3, you are almost there … 2, you are landing, gently landing … 1, you are there now. Look down at your feet. What are you wearing on your feet?"

There was a slight pause as Tim refocused in this altered state. With an amused expression, he replied a little shyly, "I'm wearing … black high heels."

I may have seen it all by now. Nothing really surprises me anymore. But back then, at the beginning of my Past Life Regression adventures, I was bewildered. My bearded man was speaking to me in a soft female tone!

The black high heels were walking down the sidewalk of a busy street. "It's New York and I'm walking on my own," Tim stated without prompting.

She was a young woman in her twenties. I asked if she was going somewhere. "I'm going to see my husband, or boyfriend?"

"Where does he live?"

"I am going to … his office, I think." She corrected me.

"Where is his office located? Can you see the name of the street? The address?" I remembered our research-based intention for this regression.

There was a long pause.

"I'm not ... there yet, but the street I'm on says 37th Street. I still have some blocks to go."

"Okay, look around you. Can you describe more of what you see?"

"It looks like I'm in the 1920s or '30s. There are lots of cars and people. And lots of traffic. Everything ... is very commercial ... It's a busy place."

"How are you feeling, walking there?"

Without hesitation, she replied, "Like I'm on top of the world."

"Feels really good, doesn't it?" I echoed. "Is it because you are going to see ... him?" Many months later, I would learn that this question was the hypnotherapist's quick assumption. It was an easy "logical" conclusion to make. But I had jumped the gun.

There was hesitation. "... Um ... A little bit of that. I don't think that's it. I think that ... it just kind of feels it's good to be me. Good to be ... alive."

"What's your name?"

"Carol."

While I sounded quite composed at the time, I was very intrigued. Tim as Carol, spoke in an extremely quiet voice during that regression session. This often happens when a person is under hypnosis because the throat muscles become very relaxed. By faintly speaking, Tim may have also contributed to Carol's soft feminine voice.

It would take a few more regression sessions with Carol's life in the 1920s/'30s for me to uncover her full story: while walking down those busy streets of Manhattan in that early afternoon, she had just concluded a secret tryst with her lover before going to meet with her husband.

Carol's husband's office was on the 6th floor of a tall building. When Carol arrived, she announced to me, "He's excited."

"What's his name?"

"… Mark."

"How old is he?"

"24 or 25."

"What does he do?"

"He is a lawyer."

"He's a lawyer, working for … a law firm?"

"Yeah … I don't know what firm." Tim as Carol had sensed that I was going to ask the name of the firm. It is not surprising. People in a hypnotic trance are highly intuitive. During hypnosis, our subconscious mind takes the driver's seat of our awareness—the subconscious being that which cradles all things memory, creativity, emotions, imagination, instinct, habits, and intuition.

I persevered, "Look around the office. Perhaps, you will see the firm's name on the door."

After a long pause, "Something *Benjamin and Son*. The firm is *his* office."

"Is it a big office?"

"About 20 or 30 people."

"Look around and you will find a calendar somewhere. On the desk or on the wall telling you exactly which year this is."

"September 1925."

"What's the purpose of meeting Mark in his office?"

"It's lunch time."

"So, is that why you are here? To have lunch with him?"

"Mark is excited. It's like he just closed a deal or something."

It became apparent that Carol was having her own trajectory of internal observation and processing. Pulling on that thread, I followed it, "What about you? What do you do Carol?"

After a brief pause, she answered, "I have fun!"

I could not help but laugh out loud. Tim the engineer would never answer a serious question that way. Yet, in a wicked way it also sounded like Tim.

"Do you work?" I asked, posing the question another way.

"No." After another little pause, "I dance."

"You dance?" That came as news to me. In his present lifetime, Tim is emphatically not an avid dancer.

"I go to clubs." There was a little smile on the corner of his/her lips. "I like to *shine*."

I was going to come back to that subject. But for now, I needed to gather more general information on the life and times of Carol. I pressed on, "Where do you live Carol?"

"We have an apartment."

"Go there now. How big is the apartment?"

Drawing a comparison to our two-bedroom apartment in Vancouver, where the session took place, Carol described her home: "It's bigger than this apartment. There's a library, two bedrooms, restroom, dining room and living room, kitchen. Just Mark and I live here." Carol's apartment had lots of dark wood furnishings. It was situated on the fourth floor, and the tops of the trees were visible from the apartment's windows. When asked the address of her home, "Chestnut Street" was the name given.

Unlike many married women where their wedding day is a significant event in their lives, Carol's never stood out in the many colourful memories from her regressions. She had grown up in New York, raised by a well-to-do family. Her father was in the shipping and transportation insurance business. At 17, Carol's parents took her to a lavish party at one of their friends or business associates. It was there that Carol first met Mark.

Mark showed immediate interest in Carol. He shared with her his plans to further his education to avoid being drafted and sent off to war. Carol was impressed by his ambition, his interest in pursuing a career in law, and building his fortune. A few days after the party, Carol received a note from Mark asking to meet with her again.

Carol's parents approved of this ambitious, hardworking man with a respectable background. Carol married Mark Benjamin at the age of 20. It was a convenient, safe, and secure arrangement for her. In

Carol's own words, the Benjamin marriage also served to get rid of her "fucking parents".

Deep down, Carol was a very conflicted woman. On the one hand, she followed the traditional dictate of the times by getting married and settling down at a young age, being a good wife, and eventually, a good mother. On the other hand, these conventional family values did not hold any great importance to her. But, Carol did not feel that she had enough agency to openly go against them. I tried to ask more questions about her family and about her husband's family. But in that first session with Carol, she could not come up with the name of "that old stuffed shirt"—a contemptuous reference to Mark's father.

Since Carol had mentioned "going to clubs" when asked what she did, I shifted her awareness to a typical clubbing moment. That was the first time the notion of a "secret" lover came up.

In the club experience, Carol was drinking and smoking with her girlfriends. Big band jazz and swing music was playing. I can completely attest to the fact that Carol's love of jazz music has traversed time and space into Tim's current lifetime.

Carol's best friend was a young lady named Denise. But on this night, the women were unhappy with one another. Denise felt Carol was misbehaving. "Maybe I'm not behaving," Carol acknowledged petulantly. "But who cares?"

"It is because you are drinking and smoking that Denise feels you are not behaving?" I inquired.

"Hmmm ... She thinks I flirt too much." Tim's eyebrows lifted suggestively, and a subtle but coy smile formed in the corner of his lips.

"In the club?"

"No. Not too much there."

"Where do you flirt?"

"With some guy in an office."

"Which office?" I thought Carol didn't work.

"He's in a big building on ... 5th Avenue?"

"Is there any specific person you flirt especially too much with?"

"Yeah ..." Tim's voice rose, and his face broke into a big smile. I could feel Carol's willingness and enthusiasm to talk about this guy.

"Who is he?" I urged.

"Rick."

"Rick ... You like him, don't you?"

"Yeah ... He's funny," Carol chuckled. "He's quite smart. He's a real deal."

"What does he do?"

"He's into stocks."

"Like a broker?"

"Hmm ... more a promoter."

"Do you just flirt with him?" I pressed further, feeling there was more to the story.

"That's what Denise thinks," Carol replied, cunningly.

"And she is already thinking that is too much?"

Instead of responding to the question directly, Carol quickly justified herself. "Well ... She doesn't know how boring Mark is."

"So how far do you go with Rick?"

"As far as I want!" Her voice was defensive now. I thought silently, *Hey easy Tim, or Carol! I am not Denise.*

Carol certainly had a way of expressing herself. She did not sound like the Tim I know. Carol was a big personality with a rebellious, somewhat self-serving, and immature nature. She would have caused me a great deal more grief than Tim ever would. But, the longer I live with Tim, the more I get to know him. And the more I am amazed at how rich the tapestry of a personality he can be; all interwoven with varying threads of tastes, likes, dislikes, emotional experiences, and other nuances of his character. When we go beyond the surface, which simply observes, "this person is like this", or "that person is like that", I can easily see the intertwined complexity of the Tim and Carol characters making perfect sense.

As I wrote this, Tim had curled up beside me on the couch, reading an e-Book on his smartphone. In that moment, a man with a moustache and beard, silently read his book and was seemingly uninterested in Carol's story. I felt very weird. It was so surreal, yet strangely satisfying.

"So, Denise suspects something is going on between you and Rick. That's why she's mad at you?"

In my work doing Past Life Regressions, I sometimes deliberately throw out one twisted question as a test for consistency and to prove authenticity of the information that comes in a session.

"I'm mad at *her*!" Carol corrected me immediately. Much of Carol's emotion came through loud and clear. It was difficult to doubt the validity of the experience. Even though, I knew Tim committed to the regression only as a birthday gift for me.

Intuitively, I felt connected to Carol's life in some way. But which character was I and what role had I played in her world?

"So, do you go out with Rick?"

"Hmm ... mostly we see each other in the afternoon or evening."

"Mark doesn't know Rick, does he?"

"No!"

"How did you meet Rick?"

"In a little diner ... He bought me a drink." Another coy smile.

"Does he know you are married?"

"Who?" Carol became alert. Why was she so sensitive towards the Hypnotherapist?

"Rick."

"No," Carol answered abruptly.

Shifting Carol's awareness yet again, I brought her forward in time to the next significant event in her life. She was at home taking care of her two children during the Great Depression. Carol still lived in the same apartment on Chestnut Street. Her daughter Anne was 6 years old and her son Mark Jr. was 4. Carol herself was now 32. And she was quite upset. Mark thought Carol ought to stay at home and tend the kids, and care for all matters pertaining to running a household. According to Mark, they could no longer afford their nanny.

"It pisses me off," Carol expressed loudly. "I'm tired of looking after the kids." Tim doesn't particularly like children. Ironically, all kids seem to naturally like him and gravitate towards him.

"So, are you having an argument?"

"No. I just ... don't like it." I felt that this was true, and that Carol probably was not openly fighting with Mark. "I know times are hard. But, why should I care? It's his job to make money!" While it was still commonplace that men were the breadwinners during the 1930s, upwards of 25% American males were unemployed or saw pay cuts of a third or more to their income. Breadlines and destitution had become the norm as many banks closed their doors, and a drought prevailed in the South.

I felt some anxiety well up in me. I paused and took a deep, steadying breath. I had a reassuring thought: *Well, if Tim in that past life was in New York, at least my Tim was not having a world war past life.*

Changing the subject, I asked, "Do you love your children?"

"Oh yeah. They are okay."

"Is Mark still working at the same firm?"

"Yeah."

"Are you still with Rick?"

"Well ... I don't know." After one of many pauses in the session, "The market crashed ..."

My heart sank. Again, I switched topics, "Are you able to keep the nanny at all?"

"No, he's gotten rid of her!" Carol was now yelling as if this outcome was utterly unthinkable.

For a while, I did not know how to move on from there. "So now you are with the two kids all the time," I repeated, hoping Carol would elaborate more.

"Yes," she simply sighed.

"And you don't like it?"

"Well, that's just not me!"

I quietly agreed. So far Carol had not sounded like a traditionally dedicated mother or housewife. She probably did not care to be a mother. I felt for her. But at the same time, I thought she was a little too stubborn. A little too self-involved.

"If the nanny were still here, what would your life be like today, Carol?"

"I'd be going out!" Carol had no qualms about showing her true feelings in front of the Past Life Regressionist. She followed that thought a little glumly, "But, there is nothing out there … Nobody is going out as much anymore."

"Do you love Mark?"

Carol searched for the right answer. "He is … a good husband, I guess. But I don't know what love is."

While I was contemplating how to move on with all of this, Carol casually added, "Anne is really a great kid. She's really smart."

"Is she six now?"

"Yes."

"Is she going to school?"

"No. She's not in school." A big sigh, but with a sense of pride, "She wants my attention."

"But she's smart, isn't she?" I echoed.

Carol must have singled out her daughter rather than her son for a reason. Until then, I had been feeling that someway or somehow, I was in Carol's life. But Carol's unsolicited comment about Anne now made me think perhaps I was Carol's daughter, Anne. I felt my energy fit. And like Anne, "being smart" has always been one of my hallmarks.

Moving Carol forward in time once more, we found her at Anne's college graduation ceremony. The year was 1947. It was two years after the Second World War had ended: a UFO had allegedly crashed in Roswell, New Mexico; India and Pakistan had gained their independence from Great Britain, and U.S. President Harry Truman marked the beginning of the Cold War by publicly initiating a war on communism and its hold in Europe.

Anne was graduating from Columbia College in New York. She had applied for Harvard University, but she hadn't yet heard back from them. Carol thought Anne was most likely going to New York University to become a lawyer.

With short hair and wearing a green suit, Carol was a proud mother at Anne's graduation ceremony. She mentioned that Mark Jr. was also growing up to be a good kid, but he was still unsure of what he wanted to do with his life.

"Not too many girls go to law school!" Carol proudly proclaimed.

"Yes. Maybe someday Anne will also work in the Benjamin & Son law firm."

"No, she doesn't want to. She wants to make it on her own." Carol chuckled, "She wants to go out and change the world."

After the graduation ceremony Carol announced, "We are going out for dinner." She said each word as if it were the most important thing.

"Which restaurant are you going to?" I remembered our purpose of later doing historical research.

"Morton's. Or something like that. Mark booked us a table. Anne's excited. She wants to go out and be with her friends, too. But she will do that after."

Mark was still at the same firm, but the firm had moved to a bigger office. The family had also moved to a bigger, brighter, and fancier apartment on Park Avenue just off Central Park. They now lived on the 8th floor, with three bedrooms, an office, a living room, a pantry, a kitchen, and a dining room.

In her 40's, it seemed that Carol had finally become a well-adapted wife and mother. Her daily life involved going to her "functions", promoting young artists, and doing charity. Carol had outgrown her party girl days. I brought up the question, "Is Denise still your best friend?"

"Huh? I haven't thought about her for a long time," answered Carol, thoughtfully.

It still amazes me how in past life regression sessions everything translates so authentically. The forty-something Carol spoke and behaved differently than that of the twenty-something Carol. She even experienced what "a long time" was as it pertained to her timeline. Despite, Tim/Carol having just been talking to me about Denise less than half an hour ago in our session.

"Did you just lose contact with her over the years?"

"Long time ago."

"How's life now?"

"Quiet. The kids are gone. I don't have much to do."

Now, that sounded like the Tim I know. He has often seemed to not have much to do ever since I met him. But he is retired, and he does not have any kids.

"And you are still with Mark?"

"Of course."

"Do you love him?"

"Oh yeah." Matter-of-factly.

Nothing much changed in Carol's life from that moment on. I could elicit no further significant events in her life. Carol died at 53, hit by a car while crossing the street in Manhattan, New York City.

Many people gathered around the body only to discover that Carol had succumbed to her injuries on impact. And here is one of the many curious things about past life regression, when asked, "Was there a funeral after the car accident?" Carol could reply, "Yes." Not only could Tim as Carol talk about this life, but s/he could also report about their death.

"How many people showed up?"

"About 75 people."

Plus, you, I thought. *As the mystery guest.*

"What was the lesson learned in living the life of Carol?" I asked.

"What seems really important in the moment has nothing to do with what turns out to be truly important in the end."

I was impressed by that reflection. "Anything else?"

"I can feel it but it's hard to put into words."

Tim's current belief system would not allow him to move any further into this inter-life awareness, the life-between-lives state. "Nothingness" was all Tim/Carol could perceive after the death of the body.

I persisted with my customary sagacity, "How do you feel in this nothingness?"

"Questions don't make sense in The Nothingness."

I am not too sure about Tim, but Carol certainly could easily outsmart me.

I was most pleased with my birthday gift.

4

The First Time, Once Again

Wednesday, July 4, 2007. Clearing off my desk, I prepared to leave the office for the day. At the last minute, the corner of the computer flashed a new email notification from "Tim Melanchuk". The name didn't ring a bell. The title however, "Blankets and Languages", put an instant smile on my face. It was as if my facial muscles knew something before my brain did.

I sat back down, slowly savouring the moment before I clicked to open the email. Tim had used the email address on the business card I had given him. It was unexpected to receive his email. At the same time, it was also the most natural thing in the world. There was no doubting, no wondering, no guessing. I simply felt something very wonderful. I was not even surprised. Things were starting to fall into place, because that was the way they were meant to be.

I opened the email:

> "Hi Kemila,
>
> "It was delightful meeting you at the Jazz Festival on Sunday. I thoroughly enjoyed our

conversation and am glad that you made use of my old blanket.

"This morning I found out that the cable network for whom we are doing our documentary on Buddhism has requested that we provide a version with Mandarin subtitles. I recall you have a fluency with languages, but I can't remember if you speak Mandarin or Cantonese. If Mandarin is in your repertoire, would you be interested in doing the translation for us? The requirement would be to translate a little less than one hour of English audio into written Mandarin in digital format. The time frame would be Feb-April 2008. We can't afford a lot, but you would be paid.

"The cable network has people that they use, and it may make more sense for us to use their people - depending upon the technical requirements for subtitle mastering and whether they can provide translation and mastering as part of one package. So, I can't promise anything right now.

"Let me know if you'd be interested. I recall you plan to visit China this coming winter, so the time frame may not work for you.

"In any case, it was good to meet you. And I would enjoy keeping in touch whether you are interested in the translation or not. I hope that your week is going well and that you have some time to enjoy this wonderful weather we are finally having.

Cheers,

Tim"

The email was sent three days after I met him. I read it again and turned off my computer. I left the office with the smile still on my face.

I replied to the email the next day. That first email exchange felt so natural, I could not help but sound like I was writing to an old friend. Indeed, that was how I felt about Tim: a new/old friend. I covered the business aspect of things first, and then praised his blanket for being so inviting. Adding, "That was a very nice and beautiful Sunday, and your blanket was definitely part of the memory."

That coming Sunday afternoon I was going to check out another outdoor concert. I knew it was going to be in the West End neighbourhood where Tim lived. Thinking it might be a good idea to ask him to join me, I extended the invitation. I finished my email light-heartedly, "And if I remember, I'll bring a blanket too."

Tim quickly responded. Unfortunately, he wasn't sure if he was going to be available that Sunday. Giving me his phone number, he welcomed me to call him when I got to the concert, telling me he would come down to join me if he was available.

It was the summer of 2007, and my first summer spent in Vancouver, even though I had moved to Canada at the end of 2002. So, I was enjoying all the activities the spectacular city had to offer. And as planned, that Sunday found me at the concert located in a park only a few blocks from Tim's place. A man resembling Tim showed up sporting a hat. I wasn't certain if it was him. The hat made him look different. But then we locked eyes and I knew it was him.

Later that afternoon I had plans to meet up with a girlfriend at Robson Square for Sunday Salsa dancing. I invited Tim to come along. He agreed to walk with me. "But I can only stay a little while. I have a conference call I need to be home for," Tim had explained.

We strolled over to Robson Square, a public plaza that is connected to the law courts, government offices and art gallery. It is a little Rain City gem that turns into an ice rink in the wintertime and is nestled neatly below ground level in the heart of downtown Vancouver. Walking into the plaza for Sunday Salsa, I almost immediately bumped into some other friends. I went off dancing with them while Tim stood awkwardly on the sidelines. Noticing his discomfort, I went to invite him onto the dance floor. "I'm afraid I have two left feet," he replied uneasily.

Much later I would recall that answer. When I asked Carol if she worked during that first regression to her life, her answer was, "I dance." Those two very different answers are still a puzzle to me. Clearly some passions and skills do not cross over through lifetimes.

Over time, Tim and I would discover that we had very different interests, in so many ways. From the beginning, what drew us together was more of the intellect, a love of travel. And maybe, jazz. In this life or the previous, always jazz.

Little did I know the summer of 2007 was to be my last summer going out dancing on a weekly or regular basis. I would soon be together with Tim.

Two days after our Sunday outing, Tim sent me another email: "I must confess to you that your conversation captivates me". He then proposed since I worked downtown, anytime I was free for lunch, coffee or drinks and a little more conversation, he would enjoy the opportunity. We began meeting up more and more. That summer I found so many events to attend and things to do, I took him up on his offer and invited him to join me. It was a busy time, and I was discovering all the beauty of the city. Especially, on those warm and dry days.

Tim's emails continued coming in every other day or so without fail. He had this unique and interesting ability to pull new conversation topics seemingly out of thin air. After we had gone to Jericho Beach together during the Folk Festival weekend, he wrote: "I had a wonderful time Friday evening. Sharing it with you made it both memorable and special. And as we're getting to know each other a little more, I'm taking greater delight in your company and conversation. So, thanks for sharing Friday

49

with me." Then he switched topics and moved on to something completely unrelated. He continued telling me how that afternoon he had picked up the latest book by his favourite Japanese author, Haruki Murakami. "And as soon as I started reading it, I wondered whether you have read any Haruki Murakami. And if so, do you like him? And which books have you read?" Tim inquired in his email. Tim must be psychic! Murakami had been my favourite Japanese author and I had read most of his books in Chinese.

Tim went on offering to lend me some of his Murakami books. It was an interesting thought—reading those books in English. I accepted the offer. The next time we met we would have more common topics. And it would be fun if we started a two-person book club.

That entire July was full of outdoor activities with and without Tim, exchanging email correspondence with him, and appointments with my realtor as I started to look for a one-bedroom condo to buy.

On the spiritual side, I got on a whole new exciting journey that "thoughts are things". It was a shocking realization for me. I had always been interested in "thoughts". Yes, I thought about my future. I thought about my past. And I thought about my friends and family. From a very young age, I had developed the habit of thinking about, or being aware of my thoughts. Lying in bed at night, I would observe my chain of thoughts and wonder how they moved and jumped from one to another all by themselves. I would sometimes try to trace their origins. Especially, when I noticed that I was having middle-of-nowhere thoughts one after another. I was utterly stunned to discover that where my thoughts had ended up had nothing to do with where they had started.

A random train of thoughts. I never thought they had any power over my life. Life was subject to luck and circumstances, things that I did not choose, such as where and when I was born, how I was brought up, how others treat me. Thoughts were passive. They were effects of my life. Sometimes thoughts had to work extremely hard to find solutions, so I could change my life—which had been my understanding until that very July.

One book I started reading that July was Abraham-Hicks' *Law of Attraction*, one of the first books that were published by Esther Hicks. Circumstances would have it that when I borrowed the book from the Vancouver Public Library, the civic workers went on strike in that very same month. So, I was able to keep the book for an unusually long time, which allowed me to read it very slowly, taking in every word, as every word shook me to the core.

Every sentence in the book struck a chord and created a resonance in me. Every paragraph woke me up a little bit more to my creative power over my life.

Thoughts were not just effects of my life. Thoughts are everything. They shape and sculpt my future! I was elated and decided to apply what I was learning from the book in my search for a condo.

One morning on my Skytrain ride into work, I was reading in the book where Abraham answers one of Jerry Hicks' many questions. This time it was about "Your Past Life". In that moment, my heart skipped a beat or two. Standing there on the crowded Skytrain, I paused from reading and looked up from the book dumbfounded. Something deep down in me had wakened. It was as if a little door to a whole new dimension had opened in me. This new dimension was to lead me to the old that I already knew. And I was calmly excited.

I took a deep breath, and I knew it was so.

It was not like I had not grown up hearing the term "previous lifetimes". Being from China, the idea of previous lives permeates the culture. However, being born during the Cultural Revolution meant we did not take reincarnation seriously anymore. It wasn't anything to consider, but simply an idea to entertain here and there. I remember many times my mother would complain how hard her life was. She would say things like, "I must have done something terribly wrong in my previous lives to have this hardship." I thought, like many people, my mother was just paying lip service to the idea. I never took it literally.

Soon after I became a Past Life Regressionist, I went back to China and visited some friends in the south. Being hospitable hosts, they took me to a grand karaoke club during my visit. While I sat there in the KTV VIP room, watching and listening to the lyrics of songs both familiar and new, I was amazed at how many times there were direct or indirect mentions of "previous lives" and "future lives" in the songs being sung. Even songs I was familiar with from over 20 years ago made mention of lives. But back then, I had not really paid much attention to the lyrics in a literal sense.

In the karaoke room, my friends sung with feigned emotions and great intensity. I wondered, how many of them truly gave a second thought to the verses they were so fervently singing? Verses like:

> *Perhaps, the hands that are now holding,*
> *Didn't have a particularly easy life before this.*
> *Perhaps, this journey, now with a partner,*
> *Will make this life even busier and tougher.*
> *So, these hands that are held,*
> *Will still accompany each other in the next life.*
> *Therefore, this journey with my partner,*
> *Will have no regrets.*
>
> —Julie Su, "Holding Hands"

Or:

> *I'd rather believe that we had a past life promise.*
> *And this life our love story will never change.*
> *I'd rather spend my whole life waiting for you to discover,*
> *That I've always been by your side and never away.*
>
> —Li Jian, "Legend"

For a number of years while I was still living in China, I wrote many travel stories for travel magazines. In one article, I was describing a mysterious experience on a misty mountaintop in the Province of Hunan:

> Clouds rise up and fall all around. Suddenly, the lake disappears, the mountain disappears, and the trees disappear. Sitting in the fog, only me is left to me. Yet, I don't know who I am or where I am ... Old stories of previous existence, and new stories of future existence all surface in this moment, intertwining with the hazy fog or cloud ...

What did I really mean in this writing? I didn't know. I knew something in me was deeply touched in that moment, being enveloped in whiteness on that mountaintop. Even though I wrote it—*previous existence and future existence*—I thought I was being more metaphorical than literal.

But that morning on the Skytrain, reading that line about past lives in the book of *Law of Attraction*, something took more solid form in me. And there it was. I did not need to go back and forth. No doubt. No questions. No need for proof. Just a complete inner knowing, I had lived before.

And so, had Tim.

5

Chestnut Street

Up to this day, Tim has rarely initiated the topics of past lives or regressions. Even though we had uncovered quite a few of his lifetimes together. Perhaps he can't make sense of it all. The engineer part of him thinks, "You can't rely on things that can't be measured." What then can he rationalize with the material that came up from our hypnosis sessions? That was easy. "I have a very vivid and imaginative subconscious mind." Or, "I read a little too many historical books."

The life of Carol seemed to be Tim's most recent life. Quite possibly we had visited that life because we had set the intention of going to a lifetime that was verifiable. But being caught in the excitement of the story itself, I soon forgot about the research and historical verification part.

Much like dreams, a lot of the details from our regression sessions quickly faded away for Tim. Sometimes I would mention some of those details to him in our conversations. And Tim would give me a blank look.

That's why I was immensely surprised one day, when Tim called me over to his desktop computer to show me an old map. Displayed on it was a Manhattan historical atlas from 1920-1924. Tim told me he had Googled the name "Chestnut Street" in Manhattan and had found there was no such street there by that name.

Was Tim disappointed or relieved by that finding? I did not know.

True to his nature, Tim dug deeper into his research and came across the website of Historic Map Works, in which he had gotten that Manhattan historical atlas from 1920-1924. I leaned closer to his computer as Tim pointed to me a tiny, short street. A street named, yes, *Chestnut St.*

What a delightful moment!

But I was more surprised by the fact that Tim was even doing this past life verification research, than I was by seeing Chestnut Street on that old map. That short little and mostly forgotten street had been unearthed from the historical dust. How had he done it?

Tim showed me how he had first found the name of Chestnut Street from the street index in the file, and subsequently brought up that little patch of the plate number 6 of the historical atlas in question. I did not know what to say. It was quite a brilliant idea to search for a historical atlas, even though I, myself had not doubted the validity of his regressed story.

I asked Tim to show me the location of the old Chestnut Street on today's Google map of Manhattan. The street was already gone, disappeared into where

James Madison Plaza is today. On the New York government park website, it cited that the land of James Madison Plaza was deeded to the City of New York in 1964. The pieces were coming together, a genealogy friend of mine once sent me a photograph taken between 1935 and 1945, of a warehouse standing in between Oak and Chestnut Streets in Manhattan, New York.

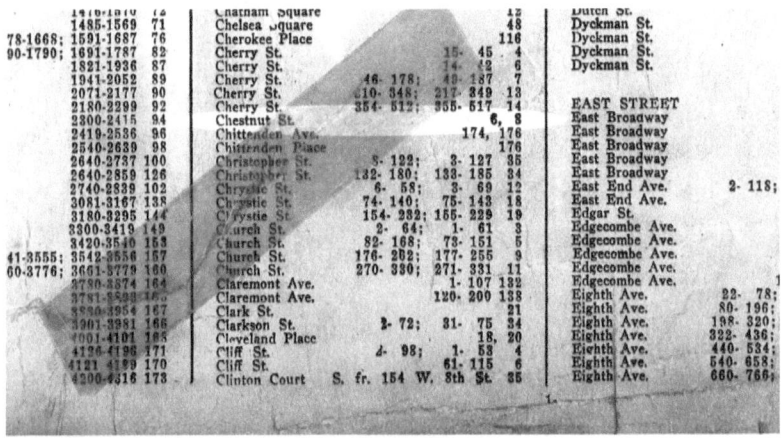

Figure 1: Map Index showing Chestnut Street on Plates 6 & 8 from: http://www.historicmapworks.com/Map/US/17544/Index+1/Manhattan+1920-1924/New+York/

I noticed that Tim had even done some Photoshop layering work, as he attempted to match the atlas of the past with the Google map of today. Tim's approach to his research, even though it silently excited me, also started to worry me. What if his conclusion was to the contrary? What if this "scientific research" proved the regressed materials invalid, and therefore, completely shut him off its actuality? He was already starting to conclude, after his initial findings, that it was impossible to be living in that area in Manhattan. I found myself justifying by bringing his attention to those cubic lines with numbers. "Obviously," I said, "those could be the residential buildings in the twenties."

During our many years together, I have learned to moderate my excitement in front of Tim. If I showed too much, or any excitement at all at the wrong time, it might translate into me pressuring him. Tim is good at doing things without being pressured. Often, his best achievements happen after he has already announced that he could not do it. When the world is not expecting anything of him, he starts to deliver.

That was why I had no idea Tim was researching land records before he had already found Chestnut Street. For me, this was the greatest discovery of the century! I tried very hard to conceal my excitement, but I didn't know to what degree I succeeded.

One evening a couple of weeks later, Tim agreed to have another past life regression session with me. However, this time he could not get into a deep hypnotic state. Perhaps Tim detected my excitement and perceived it as pressure. There were no past life scenes coming up to the surface. And knowing it was important to me, Tim wanted to "perform", which further hindered the process, because a mind that holds on to desire can prevent itself from letting go.

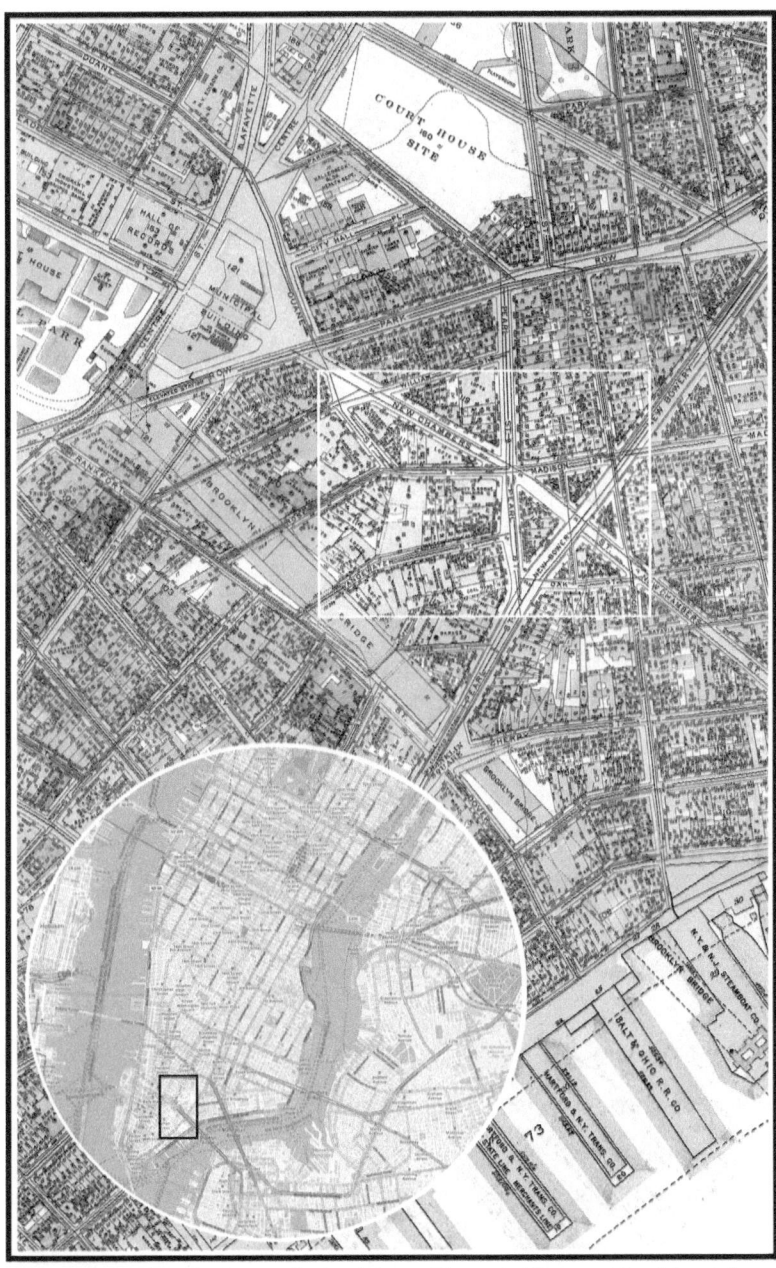

Figure 2: Historical map derived from Plates 4,6,7,8, & 40 of the Atlas. The circle inset shows the map relative to current Manhattan.

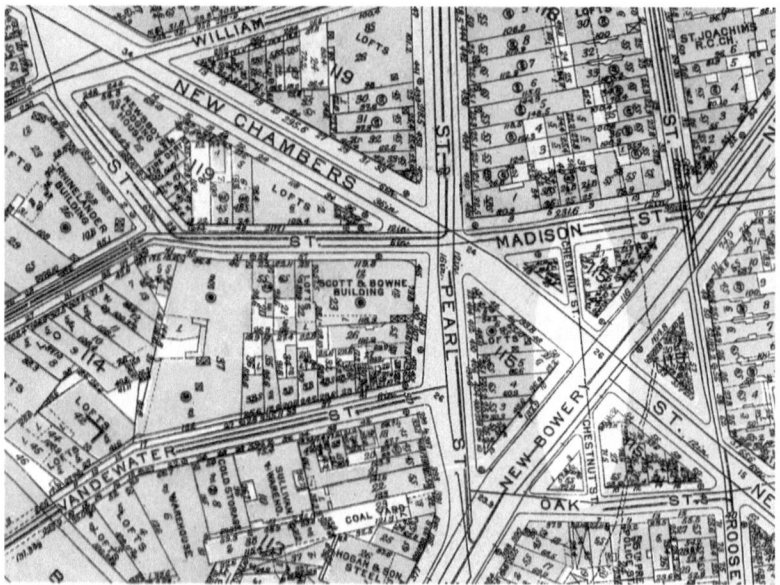

Figure 3: Enlargement of the highlighted area of the previous map. Chestnut Street runs between Madison and Oak Streets in the lower right.

We tried again to get him comfortably into a deeper hypnotic state. After a few attempts, Tim's unconscious mind took us on a Cosmic Consciousness journey, where Tim was at one with the universe. There was not much going on in his awareness other than shooting stars and galaxies. Tim enjoyed it. The sparks and the silence, offering minimum words to answer my pressing questions.

Suddenly, being completely connected, words of wisdom started flowing from his lips, "… Everything will turn out as it should. Just BE. It will turn out. Enjoy the ride …" The voice was Tim's, yet not Tim's at all. The wisdom was not just in the words, but in the whole energetic deliverance. I saw and felt the certainty in his blissfully quiet tone.

Throughout this journey, Tim's own awareness continued. He relayed how he felt a sense of familiarity in the space; he could feel the connection to eternity, the anticipation of the culmination of a cycle unfolding.

After that cosmic journey, I continued to work with Tim hypnotically on a regular basis for his insomnia. Past Life Regression was not mentioned for a while. I sometimes wondered if there were some past lives we could tap into for the sleep issue, something that plagued him during this lifetime. Yet I never suggested it. It was clear that the reason Tim had agreed to do past life regression was out of curiosity and an innate desire for exploration. Not to problem solve or to seek a cure for anything.

The next few months saw past life regression sessions with Tim as a hit or miss. There were times when Tim just "wasn't deep enough" or "couldn't see anything". The only past life regression we had was that of a young man's life. And when asked what his name was, Tim had a hard time pronouncing it - "Aarn" was the best he could come up with. Aarn was barefoot on a sandy beach on a South Pacific island. He was about 16 years old.

In those earlier days doing past life regression, I sometimes ran out of things to ask. When that happened, a handy question to pose would always be, "How are you feeling at this moment?" While most people would say "not much", especially if it was at the beginning of a session, right there on the beach, Aarn's answer to that question was very straightforward, "Horny."

That simple, one-word answer opened up the entire story of Aarn's life. He was to be party in an attack on a neighbouring island. Perhaps, it was the nervousness of going off to battle, but he wanted to have sex with his 15-year old girlfriend, Baochi. Aarn was using the passionate heat of sex to ease a dreaded feeling inside.

Aarn would subsequently become the leader of the village. He died a natural death sitting by his hut at 40-something years old, after defeating a younger man—"that fool"—who challenged his leadership. Aarn never had any children.

One day, six months later, to rouse Tim's interest again, I suggested that we do another past life regression focusing on "hot babe" Carol's life, "because the Chestnut Street you found did seem to validate her life story, and because that lifetime seemed to be both of our favourites so far."

Tim did not disagree.

6

"Tim, Keep Her"

Three weeks after our blanket encounter at the Jazz Fest, I had already shared with Tim that I felt a certain closeness towards him. I said it in the most neutral and matter-of-fact way, and it was easily understood and probably shared by him. We both felt an unexpected ease around each other. No drama, simply sharing our thoughts and feelings in a very friendly approach.

That same month of July, Tim was planning for a major life transition. At the end of the summer he was to move out of the apartment he had lived in for 13 years. Not only was he moving out, but he was moving away, and leaving a city he had lived in for over a decade. Tim first intended to go to Ontario for a month to film his documentary. Later in the year he would then travel to India for another month. After which, he would relocate to Saskatoon and housesit for five or six months while he was editing the documentary. After that? Life would just unfold as it may.

And because of that, although we were exchanging emails and meeting up with each other for festivals and lunches, Tim was reserved. As he would tell me towards the end of July, he was thoughtfully careful not to start something that he could not finish. I had noticed him being reserved. For a while I thought Tim might be gay. After all, he lived in a neighbourhood that was known for its gay community, and I never heard him talking about women. It was also possible, I thought, that he was committed to someone.

Whatever it was, I was not the least bit bothered or concerned. It was a magical month in my life. Tim moving or staying, I was enjoying his company. Looking back, sometimes I wish that magical sense of living in the moment had always been there for me.

I started to fantasize how Tim would react if I told him my theory that there were past lives, that we had known each other "before". I felt the excitement of this fantasy. So, emailing Tim on the same day I had read about past lives from Esther Hicks, I wrote: "The closeness I feel towards you is unexplainable. Well, I actually came across some new ideas this morning. You won't believe it, not at least until we've had some wine, and you listen to me explain."

For Tim, my bubbling excitement transmuted into a deep sense of curiosity, and his response made me fall down laughing: "I would love to hear about this, although, I'm a wee bit worried that you might say that I remind you of your father." Without the frame of past lives, that was as far as his imagination could go, I supposed.

Maybe Tim was referring to the fact that he was over ten years older than me. But ironically, my father and I are not that close. He provided for our family and worked hard, he was physically there, but emotionally and mentally he was a distant figure. We get along well enough and interact fine when I visit, but there is often a reserve between us. It may be that we are so different that I failed to really understand my father. Or perhaps, my father has never given me an opportunity to understand him.

The next time I saw Tim, we took the SeaBus—a passenger-only, public transit ferry that crosses Burrard Inlet from downtown Vancouver—to North Vancouver and the Caribbean Festival there. Not over a glass of wine as promised, as Tim was too curious to wait, he asked me about the idea I had wanted to share. I told him my theory that we had met each other in at least one lifetime before this one. Tim did not know what to make of it. We were sitting on the grass, him leaning back on a little knoll behind us, with hands interlaced behind his head, looking up at the blue sky. He replied, "I really like the sound of it. But my engineer mind has a hard time accepting it."

The following day Tim's parents would drive a long distance to come and stay with him for the next ten days. He was anxious about managing the stress of packing for his move, while spending time entertaining his parents. Tim expressed his desire to see me as much as our time could allow. "I wish I had met you a year ago." He wrote in an email, "I'm wondering when I will get to see you again. It seems that I have such little time before I have to go to Ontario for filming. And that scares me a little since, in this life anyway, I haven't known you as much as I'd like. So, I'd like to see you and talk with you …" Tim's heartfelt message gave me the chance to tell him that so far that summer was the best summer of my life.

Of course, the best summer of one's life could not be complete without a fireworks display. The annual Celebration of Light fireworks show and competition is normally held during the last week of July and the first week of August, at English Bay, close to where Tim lived.

I mentioned to Tim in a follow-up email, that I was going to watch the fireworks. Tim said he and his parents were going too, so he suggested I come over for dinner after work and together we could all walk down to English Bay afterwards. I gladly accepted and arrived with a bottle of wine in tow. Tim's parents were both very chatty and kind, and I made fast friends with his father. I suppose that is what happens when an Aquarius meets a Gemini. We started teasing one another almost instantly. It was like we were old friends, where there were no filters or secrets from each other.

Tim's parents had been married to each other for most of their lives. "After over fifty years with her," his father told me, "I just made my decision…"

"What decision was that?" I could not contain my curiosity.

"That she's a keeper." Tim's father said cheekily.

"Wow!" I felt a need to dramatize it for him, but at the same time I was genuinely intrigued, "That must be the most serious decision ever, to take you over fifty years to make!"

Tim was busy barbecuing, and his parents and I were enjoying some wine. While carrying some food from the kitchen to the barbecue on the balcony, Tim's father interrupted him and bluntly said, "Tim, I like her. You should keep her." Tim blushed. Luckily, he was on his way out. I felt a little embarrassed too. A moment later, Tim said sotto voce to his father, "I'm not sure if she's mine to keep."

We had dinner and went down to the bay for a fantastic firework show. Earlier that same day I had received an email from Tim, he apologized for not being completely forthcoming with me for a decision he had made. I had read the email but had not had a moment to respond to it before showing up at his apartment. The beginning of August was the time Tim needed to give the management of his building one-month notice for moving out. That was when Tim had changed his plans without telling me. He decided to keep the apartment for another three months, even though he would be paying September's rent while he was out of town.

Again, Tim found it easier to express himself via email:

> "The reason I didn't tell you, leads me to the real reason I need to apologize. I wanted to say this in person. But, as you have noticed, I can start thinking and my head goes around in circles, and sometimes nothing gets said. I do

think a lot and sometimes it does get in the way of what I feel. Throughout the last month, getting to know you, and knowing that I was leaving, I have been conscious of keeping some distance from you at times. This has been easy, because I am naturally a shy person, especially with women. It has been quite a while since I have been with anyone. And as time has gone by, the more nervous I have been and the more reserved I have become ...

"Whether I can ever overcome my nervousness or not, I don't know. But I absolutely want, from the core of my being, to at least be able to express my feelings to you. You have brought me great joy this last month. You make me look at the world differently, and better in so many ways. You make me laugh and my heart smile. I want you to know that. One of the main reasons that I am staying here a little longer, is my hope that we now have August to get to know each other a little more, without my rushing and packing and stressing. And where I will try and be more open. Please help me do that and forgive my failures.

"Now, if this hasn't been too typically male, or too typically Canadian or just plain scary ...

It was late after the fireworks, and I went home after midnight to reply to Tim's email:

> "Yes, I am not yours to keep. No, not yours to keep, unless you want to."

7

"I'd Like Another Drink"

After his research on Chestnut Street, a proposed session targeting Carol's life again, meant that Tim's interest was genuinely higher than usual. I wanted to make sure that this time he would go deep enough into a hypnotic trance. So, I used a *Seven Plus Minus Two* confusion induction to put his thinking mind in the backseat. In such an induction, a Hypnotherapist constantly shifts the client's attention around, challenging them to focus on five to nine things, such as the temperature on their skin, the sound of the hypnotist's voice, their breathing pattern, the comfort of their arms, the heaviness of their eyelids ... until they get overloaded and drop into a trance. I was giving Tim suggestions that his subconscious mind knew, and was willing to take us, on an interesting journey; that his subconscious mind had started the preparations for this journey while we were still talking, and whether it was imagination, fantasy, or memory, it would happen. I guided him into the trance, "The less you work on it, the faster it will come to you."

Tim's father had passed away several years earlier, and his 89-year old mother had just paid us a visit. Together we had all driven to East Vancouver to visit the old neighbourhood where they used to live for the first eight years of Tim's life. We had seen their old house, so I decided to incorporate that into building his confidence in remembering, and into his unconscious agreement with this work:

"You can remember a gentle happy moment in the past week ... when your mother visited ... If you can remember anything about it, this finger will lift ... That's how you remember everything. You don't need to work on it. Memories simply come to you when you are very relaxed. Remember the day you went back to the old house where you lived as a child ... It is still there ... Your childhood life in that house ... If any happy memory comes to your mind, as they will, lift that finger again ... That's right. Thank you. And what does it feel like, look like, sound like, smell and taste like, that early, early memory? ... Memories always come to you easily and naturally when you go deep into trance ... Now!"

Gradually I took Tim into the past life. He landed in a bar, drinking.

"Are you there with someone else or are you alone?"

"I think I'm alone right now."

"How are you feeling there?"

"Excited."

Being alone and excited? I asked, "Are you expecting someone?"

"No. It's fun to be here."

I thought "here" meant the bar Carol liked frequenting. "Do you come here often?"

"First time."

I was not sure what to ask next. Even though we set about traveling to Carol's life again, I had to be cautious, as sometimes the subconscious mind will have its own agenda.

Tim volunteered the next piece of information, "In Havana."

"Havana?" What is going on? "Do you live there? Or are you visiting?"

"Visiting."

"What's your name?"

"… Carol?" The tone was rising as if inquiring, *'How do you not know that?'*

"Ah hah, you are in Havana!" All the initial confusion was gone. Now it made sense. I must have sounded like I had just met an old friend, in that past life regression. But I did, didn't I?

I asked, "Did you go to Havana by yourself?"

"No. With him."

"And *he* is not with you now?"

"Not right now."

"What's his name?"

"Rick."

Rick? Interesting.

"Do you know where he is now?"

"In the hotel."

I have been to Cuba. I wondered where they had stayed. Seeking a piece of verifiable information, I asked, "Which hotel is it? You remember the name of it."

"Ingla … terra?"

Hotel Inglaterra? I had not heard of it. But later when I searched online, I discovered that the hotel is still operational to this day. Even more so, Hotel Inglaterra—named for England—with its elegantly classic design is Havana's oldest hotel, having opened its doors in 1844 in central Havana. I made a mental note that next time Tim and I decided to go to Havana, I would know where to stay.

I continued with my line of questioning, "What does Rick do?"

"He's in the stock market."

"Whose idea was it to go to Havana on vacation?"

"Mine." Carol's voice suggested that she was a little drunk, "But, I let him think it was his."

It was October or November of 1927. Carol and Rick were spending two weeks in Havana.

They had taken a 2-day train ride from New York to Florida, and then a boat from Miami, Florida to Havana, Cuba. To get away for this out-of-town tryst, Carol had come up with a story, for her husband Mark, of going to Georgia with a girlfriend of hers for a couple of weeks to visit her girlfriend's grandparents.

I wanted Carol to dive deeper into the full story. "Now move forward in time," I instructed, "to the moment when you get back to New York. What's happening next?"

"I don't want to go back to New York!" Carol raised her voice. In that moment, the Tim part of the personality was completely gone. Well, it sure sounded like a lot of people I know, unwilling to end a vacation. But what could we do now, in our session?

I found the first part of the conversation with Carol to be really unsteady. Carol seemed to be guarded, resistant, or plain uncooperative.

Or maybe she was just too drunk?

There was a moment I thought, perhaps instead of being Anne in Carol's life, I was Mark. I felt an unusual resistance towards me, the past life regressionist, as Carol was particularly challenging to speak with during that session.

I sighed, "So what do you do? You stay in Havana forever?" I was not sure what I could do with the direction of this session. This Carol was so stubborn and belligerent. "What about Rick? Doesn't he have to work? He can't stay here forever I'm sure."

"He did say I could stay here as long as I want. We don't have to go back."

I was at loss, "So where should we go from here?" I asked. I figured if she wanted to direct the session, it was fine with me.

But Carol had her usual cunning way of answering, "I want to go to Paris!"

What?!

"How about Rick?"

With a sigh, "… He's not so much into it."

"So, you are not going to Paris?"

"I don't know what I'm going to do." I felt Carol would be happy to simply stop answering the rest of my questions all together.

I decided not to indicate where and how she should move forward in the session, but simply give her the general command, "Now Carol, listen carefully, we'll move forward in time, moving forward in time, to the next significant event in this life as Ca—"

"That's what *he* always says!" Carol interrupted me, still sounding drunk.

"What is it that *he* always says?"

"Always trying to reason it."

"What does he reason?" I was not sure who Carol was referring to anymore. Was it Rick, or her husband Mark?

"Always not what I want, but what he says!—'Carol, be reasonable.' Why do I have to be reasonable?" Her voice was so loud that I wasn't sure if her argument was directed towards me or not. But I kept my composure.

"So, tell me Carol: what is it that *you* want?"

Silence. I asked again.

"Well, I tell him what I want, but I'm not completely sure if what I tell him *is* what I want."

So complicated. Or simply confused? I was frustrated. I wondered if Carol could just tell *me*, the past life regressionist, what she wanted.

It eventually turned out that Carol was referring to Mark, who always talked about family stuff, career, work …

I tried to move Carol forward in time again, "Now Carol, listen carefully, we are going to …"

"You sound like Mark, 'Now, Carol, listen!'" Carol interrupted me again.

I told myself to be patient, especially since I seemed to be dealing with someone who was drunk. So that was it. I must be Mark in that lifetime. Given the fact Tim was so diligent in finding Chestnut Street in the historical atlas, I wanted Carol to confirm it one more time, so I asked, "Where do you live Carol?"

"New York. Manhattan."

"In an apartment?"

"Yes."

"Is there a name for the apartment building, or address?"

After a 20-second pause, Carol answered, "I'd like another drink."

"Where are you? At home?"

"Still in Havana!" Carol announced triumphantly.

"What's going on?" I was more than a little frustrated trying to decipher everything.

Carol's answer followed, "Music … Dancing …"

The story seemed to be going nowhere.

Knowing it probably would not work as I was dealing with an inebriated Carol, but for the lack of better direction, I attempted once again to get Carol to tell me the apartment address. After a minute-long pause, she simply asked back, "Why do *you* want to know?"

As far as I know, nobody has ever asked that question of their past life regressionist!

I gave up.

"Carol, why did you marry Mark? You don't seem to love him that much."

"It's complicated." It seemed the more honest answer would need to come up in a later session when Carol was more sober.

I wanted to ask more about her daughter, Anne. I wanted to pinpoint *my* identity in Carol's life, but Tim was yawning and saying, "I'm tired."

Tim/Carol were likely drained from the session's outpour of emotions, after a night or day, of drinking. I slipped in one more question, "Carol, how's your sleeping?"

"I sleep fine, generally. When I was younger, I was wild, so sleeping was a little troubled. But it's fine after I had children."

It didn't sound like Tim's sleeping issue had anything to do with that past life. The session ended. Something had been quite off in that session. It was unsettling. I had lost the flow, the rapport, and the nice momentum of the first session. It seemed I had asked the wrong questions at the wrong times in this second session of Carol's life. Carol seemed provoked and reactionary towards many of my questions. Or perhaps she was simply too drunk to engage well.

I *must* be involved in that life. I could feel it, though I could not yet put my finger on exactly who I was. At that moment, however, I was quite sure that I was not Anne.

8

The One Who Travels

The apartment that Tim intended to keep for only three more months back in 2007, we still live in to this day. Life has its own ironic plan for everything. It is easier and more fulfilling to follow life's path for us than to resist it. Even though the mind generally does not quite understand this magical simplicity of life itself.

Things continued to unfold in their natural course. A week after the Celebration of Light fireworks, Tim expressed himself much more openly:

> "I know what I want. I want to create, and I want a deep meaningful connection with someone special. You. I may not know the best things to do or to say all the time. And I may sometimes do or say the opposite of what is best. All I can do is to try and to learn. And see where that process takes me with you. A week ago, my eyes opened. I'm here. Let's see the journey and experience what we can have."

One reason people choose to get together, is that they find it easy to be themselves in the presence of the other person. This had been the case for me with Tim. The month of August flowed smoothly. Tim and I continued to hang out on the beach after work and on weekends. We went camping near Squamish, a mountain town north of Vancouver, and had a wonderful evening by the campfire under the full moon. Both of us were aware that he was going away soon for a month-long trip, so we decided to spend as much time together as possible.

When September came, Tim left me the key to his apartment, packed all his camera and audio gear, and went on his first trip to film the documentary. We continued with our email correspondence and phone calls when we could—social media and smartphones were still not a part of our everyday world. Tim stayed at the home of his friend and documentary partner in the small cottage-country city of Peterborough, Ontario. His friend did not have home internet and Tim had to go to a café to read and write emails.

That same month, I became a Canadian citizen. And my realtor helped me find a one-bedroom condo, a short walk along the seawall from Tim's apartment, in the same West End neighbourhood.

No matter where I was or what I was doing, I kept an ongoing conversation with Tim in my head. He wrote me saying he did the same. Once after we spoke on the phone, he wrote, "hearing your voice brings a little song of joy to my spirit".

In October, Tim came back from his trip to Ontario, just in time to help me move. Now that we seemed to be "officially" in a relationship, I started to meet some of Tim's friends.

I was changing. Finding a new spiritual dimension was extremely exciting to me. It was also interesting how Tim and spirituality came into my life at the very same time, even though Tim did not—and still doesn't—care about spirituality the way I do. When you love someone, it is so easy to assume that person has the same ideas and tastes as you do in just about everything. I was genuinely surprised that with some of the words of wisdom, commonly known as "New Age" thoughts, which resonated with me so clearly and dearly, Tim could not feel anything at all, to the point he'd say he couldn't understand it. I sincerely could not understand why he could not understand it. Wasn't it all in plain English?

Mid-November came and Tim was going away again, first to Italy for two weeks to visit a friend, and then to India to continue filming the documentary until after Christmas. During the long days without Tim, I read, and read, and read, in my new condo, while still putting new furniture together. All my evenings and weekends were spent reading. I had read two or three books a week, none of them fiction. I found it quite amusing. Here I was, reading all these "New Age" books, that more or less were derived from ancient Eastern philosophy, much of it originating from India, and caring for every bit of it. And there Tim was, the man who was on his way to India, to film a documentary about Buddhism, and not caring much about spirituality at all. Life sure does have its contrary ways for us.

On December 1, I wrote to Tim:

> "The first snow of the year in Vancouver has come this morning. It found me reflecting in front of the window. From the beginning of summer, until now the beginning of winter, I've been through a lot and every step is clearly marked in my memory. It's been a wonderful time. I somehow feel right now I'm

growing into a new stage, though not exactly sure what it is."

Being in Italy, Tim responded with more romantic expression:

"I imagine you with me whenever I am feeling happy. Yesterday I went to a little town south of here that I had not been to before. The sun was shining, and it was warm, and I sat on a little bench at a bar. It faced the bay and the water, and I shared it with a couple of old Italian men. We were all sipping grappa, and I felt very Italian. My thoughts idly drifted from one thing to another, but they always came back to you, as they always do.

"You are my heart. I don't know if I will ever be able to express in words how much you mean to me; how beautiful you are to me. Your spirit is always present with me, giving me warmth. I am always imagining you beside me, in the warmth of the sun's embrace. I love you. Every single part of my being is in love with you."

Tim would soon be in India. He did not know then that he had at least one past life in India—a devoted man in his sect from a very young age. Tim enjoyed India. His first sight of the Ganges was akin to a festive carnival, with several Pooja ceremonies going on, each with 6 to 8 people performing.

He described it in an email:

"Along the Ganges here it is magical, spiritual, and simply weird at times. Bells are ringing incessantly, stands of candles being waved in the air by the performers, incense, and smoke, wafting through the air. The bells were attached to scaffolding above the performers with long strings reaching to the front of the audience, where the ringers sat, pulling on the strings which danced against the black night sky.

"Watching families take their spiritual cleansing in the river, seeing the bodies burning on the shore, fills me with a sense of wonder. And feeling like a stranger in a strange land. I think you would be fascinated here.

"Yesterday evening, after returning to our hotel after dinner near the river, approaching from the distance, I heard raucous drums and loud music start outside. At first, I thought that a festival had started a short distance away and I feared getting a decent sleep. But the sound became louder, as if coming closer, and then looking out my window I saw colourful lights appear above the plants in the garden, which separates our hotel from the street in front.

"Knowing sleeping would be impossible, even with earplugs, I went to see what was going on and discovered a wedding procession, weird and wacky and joyous, a somewhat bizarre and magical blend of technology and culture as if from a slightly bent parallel universe.

> "Big loud generators on wheels powered some switchboard like thing as if from some early sci-fi movie. Out of that ran cables powering wedding cake shaped masses of flashing lights, carried by people, forming a circle round the wedding party as they moved slowly down the street. Bagpipes, horns, and drums created a strange brew of music.
>
> "The brothers of the groom asked me to join them. I was tired and declined, but a big smile lit my face and there was joy in my heart. For some reason, that small little procession made me feel more alive and present than I was able to down at the magic of the Ganges."

I would have loved travelling to India with Tim. I love travelling, but I have not been to India. I could feel my heartbeat in response to Tim's illustration and his choice of words. Yet strangely, I was not really longing for him as if something were missing. I felt content.

Tim continued his journey in India. When he was not writing to me, he kept his thoughts in his journal:

> "Sitting now in a tourist restaurant off one of those narrow twisty streets behind the river, ordering a banana lassi, naan, and butter chicken, and hoping that once eating, I remain healthy.
>
> "Midday spent exploring along the Ganges, absorbing the sense of the place. At times, a sense of the spiritual overtakes me, and I wonder what it would be like to have faith, to believe in something. Instead of faith, I have Kemila. Thoughts of her are

never far. And is not love, similar to faith? Both being beyond reason and attachment to something other than oneself.

"Watching bodies burn, feeling alien, fearing death, at least here. And that too brings thoughts of Kemila. I first rationalized her sense of being alone at the end of her life as simply her outliving me, always believing, having faith, that we will remain together. But over the last weeks, since I left Vancouver, I have been overcome with the sense of obligation to outlive her, so that her prophesy is false. But mostly so that she has love at the end of her life, of being wanted, that was missing at the beginning of her life."

Life had changed so much for me that I had almost forgotten that prophesy I had shared with Tim. It was about the beginning of my life. In my family, I was born as an unwanted girl, instead of a highly desirable boy. I did not receive enough attention growing up, and I thought I would mostly die alone.

Aside from his filming project, it seemed Tim kept having his own unexpected sweet and magical moments travelling in India. On his last night's stay in Varanasi, he again went to watch the Pooja ceremonies by the Ganges, where he met a flower-candle girl. She taught him how to make wishes and set the lit candles afloat. Riding back through the crowds in his cycle rickshaw, somehow and in some way, Tim knew that I was blessed by Mother Ganges.

Tim would have enjoyed the trip differently had he not met me prior to that. As it was though, at the same time as he was experiencing the wonders of India, part of him was counting down the days till he came back home to Vancouver. As it happened, the filming had gone so smoothly that Tim was left with more days without an agenda than anticipated, and found himself wishing that he could leave earlier. But he could not change the flight without paying too much of a penalty. So, his Eastern journey continued:

"Bodhgaya, Dec. 14, 2007

I haven't been writing. Bodhgaya is an ugly little town that gets packed with tourists/pilgrims this time of the year. For several days, I have been struggling with a cold and itching from the bites of bed bugs. Yesterday I felt lost and disconnected, a feeling I sometimes get when I observe a crowd belonging to something, and I long to be part of something other than myself. And I started missing Kemila hugely.

"Kemila's latest email told me that she loved me. That both warms my heart, and yesterday, feeling alone and fragile, made me scared that she's fallen for someone as broken as me.

"Every muscle aches. But for some reason, a smile comes easily today, where yesterday all that I wanted was to cry. It is difficult to let go of the bad thoughts in my head, even as I recognize them and know that I should ..."

That month, as Tim struggled to balance the marvels of his travels with a longing for connection, I was busy experiencing new things in my new country Canada, like going about to

Christmas parties with friends and colleagues. While Tim was touring in a country with the least amount of Christmas atmosphere. He and his documentary partner had hired a car and were driving across central India, through picturesque little towns, and walking along rivers by old temples:

> "I am in Bodhgaya now. This is where Siddhartha gained enlightenment and is the holiest place in Buddhism. I have spent the last several hours walking around and sitting by the main temple here, surrounded by monks. There is chanting everywhere. I have been trying to meditate a little."

Christmas Eve, Tim spent it sleeping outside beneath the full moon:

> "… dreaming of you, in the yard of someone just outside a little village. In the village is this old well, in the shape of an inverted pyramid, with stairs cascading down the insides. Watching the shadows change the patterns under the full moon was enchanting."

It was all too surreal.

9

Ocean Waves, Anciently Young

A month after our troubled second past life regression in Carol's life, I was able to talk Tim into yet another regression session. In it, Tim traveled to a male's life in 18th century Canada. His name was Jean LaChance. Armed with a rifle, he was a soldier fighting against the government. Jean died on the battlefield at the age of 33.

Upon his death, Jean realized what a wasted life he had led. No "good cause" is worth dying for. And it dawned on him that instead of dying on that battlefield, he could have run away and started over.

I did not know how many lives Tim had lived. If possible, I wanted to know them all. Nothing could fascinate me more than that, especially with the person I am so close to.

It was towards the end of September, the days were getting much shorter, and the weather was cooler. One day, after several cloudy days, the sun came out. I suggested to Tim, "Why don't we try a past life regression out in nature, like on the beach?"

Now that I had used up my easier tactics, I was becoming more creative in my approach to getting Tim to agree to having regression sessions. This one however was new, even to me. That idea intrigued Tim and he was once again under my spell.

We packed blankets and went to a little patch of beach between English Bay Beach or First Beach, and Second Beach. I had fondly dubbed it One and a Half Beach.

I settled Tim down by a log, and covered him with a blanket, making sure he was comfortable and warm enough. I used a *Full-Length Mirror* induction—a hypnotic technique where the individual imagines seeing his/her reflection in a full-length mirror—to get to a life that he had lived. This was for the pure fun of exploration. Even I didn't have any agenda other than that.

Upon entering a past life, the three questions a Hypnotherapist normally asks are:

"Is it daytime or nighttime?"

"Is it inside or outside?"

"Are you alone or are you with someone?"

It was daytime and Tim was outside, alone.

"Where are you?" I asked.

"There is miles and miles of beach."

Interesting, I thought. This must be an environmental influence. With the sound of ocean waves crashing against our sandy beach, it must be easy for Tim to travel to a beach scene.

Just as we had started the regression, a group of people had wandered over to the same small beach. I must have looked strange to them, kneeling beside a man who was lying there with his eyes closed, my ear to his mouth—Tim's voice was barely audible over the ocean sounds. The mixed group of both men and women were led by a young lady. She seemed to be their yoga instructor or meditation guide. The class settled in and started their practice. Watching them, I realized I actually looked less weird than they did. And they did not seem at all concerned about the two of us on the beach, either. I continued to give Tim suggestions, in an effort to tune out the instructor's loud voice in the background.

"Miles and miles of beach." I repeated, half yelling over the rhythmic breaking of the waves. "What else do you see there?"

"Just beach. It is a cloudy day."

"What time of the day is it?"

"It's afternoon."

"Do you see other people on the beach?"

"No. Pretty much no one."

"What are you doing there?"

"Walking."

"By yourself?"

"Yeah. I like to walk on the beach."

"You do enjoy it, don't you?" I echoed. "Which season is this?"

"It's Autumn."

"What are you wearing?"

"I'm wearing pants, a blue and white jacket, and white runners."

"How old are you?"

"About 50."

At the beginning of each Past Life Regression session, I like to focus on the flow itself, rather than any detailed information. Of course, my mind wanted to know it all: name, gender, all the stories. But it is easier to allow the information to flow organically, especially at the beginning. When the flow has been established, it then becomes easier to ask identifying information.

I continued the flow, "So this afternoon, you are walking on the beach, and you like it. After your walk, where do you go?"

"Back to the house."

"Now go back to the house. Tell me what the house looks like."

"It's white with two stories and has a grey roof."

"What's happening in the house. Is anybody else there?"

"No."

"You live alone, then?"

Tim took a long pause before answering, "I don't live here. I'm just staying here … for a while. I often come up here on my own for a couple of weeks."

"Is it a beach house?"

"Yeah."

"You said you stay there. But, it's not your house?"

"Yes. It's my house."

I had been caught making assumptions, again. "Now go about the house. Look and see if you can find a calendar anywhere." I figured I could at least find out what year we were in.

"No. I came here to get away from everything."

"I see." That was all I could say, even though I did not fully understand.

"I walk … and … I paint." Tim volunteered some information, and his voice seemed surprised, as if he discovered something. "I have a studio here!"

"What do you paint?"

"The beach, the ocean, the trees, the scenery. Landscapes."

"After you finish painting a piece, do you put your signature on the painting?"

"Yeah. I sign with my initials."

"What are your initials?"

"C. C."

"What does the first C stand for?"

"Carol."

"Carol?" My voice could not help but reveal a surprise. What is going on here? Are we back to Carol's life again? I asked, "What's the second C?"

"Clark."

I thought Carol's last name was Benjamin … Is this a different Carol? What were the odds?

"Carol Clark. Do you also sign the year after you finish a painting?"

"No. I don't."

"But you do know which year you are in now, don't you Carol?"

"It's 1952."

I handed Tim a notepad and a pen, and asked Carol to sign on it the same way she normally would after finishing a painting. Tim took the pen and paper, and artistically decorated the same letter twice. Days later I asked Tim to sign C. C. pretending as if it were his own initials. Tim's version of the initials proved to be significantly different than that of Carol's.

"So, Carol, how are you feeling now that you are back at your house after walking on the beach?"

Carol took a long pause, "Content is not quite the right word, but it's close."

"So, you walk, and you paint, are they pretty much what you do every day here?"

"Yeah. And read in the evening. There's a fireplace. We will close the house up soon, though."

"Close up? Are you going to sell it?"

"God no! It's been the family house forever. We've had it for years. We just don't keep it open in the winter."

Something was obvious for Tim/Carol here but not me. Maybe I was being a little daft, or I was just distracted by the yogis beside me. I hadn't connected things yet.

"Where do you spend the rest of the year?"

"Manhattan!" Carol's tone was surprised that I even asked it.

"Go back to Manhattan now …"

"Oh! I don't want to…" Just like that Carol in Havana. Still assertive, even when sober.

I needed to find out where exactly Carol was staying, "How far are you now from Manhattan?"

"Not that far. 20 miles? I don't know. I'm not great with distances." Tim is super great with distances. Maybe they are right when they say men are good with distance and directions, and women are not, even when they are the same soul.

"Is it on the mainland, or an island?"

"Both are an island, but when you drive there are bridges and there's not much distinction between island and mainland, you know?"

"I see. So, you drove there. How long does it take driving here from Manhattan?"

"Depending on traffic. Three hours?"

"Your paintings. What do you do with them? Do you sell some?"

"Mostly it's a hobby. I've given some to friends."

"You said you don't want to go back to Manhattan. What's there waiting for you when you drive back?"

"Mark … and life … you know … everything."

"Your children. They are not home?"

"No. They are off to school."

"Is Mark busy?"

"I guess he's busy. He still has the firm. That's what he does. Managing old clients. Things are well established now. Everything is … I don't want to say easy, but, orderly."

"How about your life Carol? Do you have any friends?"

"I have lots of friends." Carol sounded bored.

"Any particular close ones?"

Another long pause, "I don't get any strong feelings about that."

"Carol, do you keep a journal or a diary?"

"No. I like reading, not writing."

We had never explored Carol's earlier years prior to marriage. I thought now might be a good opportunity to do so. I counted Carol back to an earlier time, an interesting memory in her childhood. Lo and behold, Carol took us back to 7 years old. She was playing with her older brother and younger sister … on a beach! The very same Long Island beach, but it was summertime. The children were building a sandcastle. I asked 7-year-old Carol how she felt, and she just giggled.

Carol was born on March 15, 1902, and grew up in Manhattan, New York. Her father's name was Charles Clark and her mother's Elizabeth Clark. Carol had an older sister, Liz and a younger brother, Chuck. They were a typical American family of the time, where "Daddy makes money and Mommy spends it."

Mark the husband was three years older than Carol. I could not think about anything else to ask. Talking with this self-content, well-respected, 50-something-year-old Carol, it did not seem very appropriate for me to ask about Rick, her old paramour, and the main character in our last session. I took Carol to her last day again. I wanted to know the details of that day, what had been going on, what had she been thinking and feeling, and how exactly she died.

There was nothing special about the day to start with. Carol had gotten up in the morning not knowing that it was to be her last day in that life. She was scheduled to attend a lunch meeting, which had something to do with the charity work she was involved in. But Carol was never to arrive.

On her way to the meeting, Carol took a cab to a bookstore first. Browsing books was something Carol liked to do. It was a hobby Tim shares. Before meeting me, Tim didn't have a library card. He always bought books to read. And he had floor to ceiling shelves full of books and books.

She had intended to walk from the bookstore to her meeting. But the moment Carol stepped out of the bookstore—"I guess I just wasn't paying attention." A car hit her at the intersection. People had gathered around; it all had happened so quickly.

I sighed. How many times has Tim looked at his phone for directions while crossing a street when we travel? And how many times has it made me nervous that he was completely relying on other drivers' behaviours for his own safety as a pedestrian?

"What is your last thought before you die, Carol?"

"Of Mark and Anne. Mark was such a good man, and I am not going to see what Anne achieves. She's going to do something."

"What achievements? Will she get her doctorate degree?"

"It's not so much the education, but her attitude. She has the willpower and determination."

"Maybe you can become her guardian angel, still looking over her." I didn't receive a yes or a no answer to that magical idea, though. It was 2011 when that beach session took place. Anne could, I calculated, have been in her 90's if she were still alive. As for Mark, it would take two more years for Tim to hesitantly identify who he may be in his current life, a lawyer and good friend of his.

We still could not go to any further afterlife explorations this time, even though I tried.

"Things just end. I'm about to cease to exist." Carol was gone. But what then? Who still exists? I know existence will not cease to exist, otherwise it would not be "existence", would it?

I continued, "You still exist. You just exist in a different form, or maybe formless now."

"A very light form."

"Yes, a very light form." It delighted me that Tim didn't dismiss what he was experiencing, "And maybe that's your true nature." I continued, "The density of being human is because of the heavy costume we put on when we incarnate. The heaviness in this physical life also creates the idea of time. With the sense of time, we can experience 'change', 'growth', 'advance', and 'progress', in this game of life.

"In this light state, we can realize it is actually our true nature. Being light is not to cease to exist. Like a drop of water, with heat, it become steam. It still exists, just in a lighter form. And we exist in awareness."

And Tim's awareness came back after the death of Carol. I brought him out of his hypnotic state. We were now alone on the beach.

And the ocean waves continued the crash of their ancient song.

10

Trial Times

As 2008 was arriving, the time finally came that Tim and I would be living in the same city, and in the same neighbourhood. It was the time we had looked forward to for so long. I continued with my self-discovery book reading journey. Yet, I was met with huge and unanticipated resistance from Tim when I tried sharing my new "discoveries" with him.

I love change, and always embrace it. In fact, it is a lack of change that can scare me. I realized that in order to become the person I wanted to be it was not the world, but myself that needed to grow and change. After reading many books over the summer, I understood that it was mostly my thoughts that needed to shift. Thoughts, after all, are everything.

Since Tim had come into my life, I felt it would be nice to have him onboard with me on this journey. I could not understand what his resistance was about. Why would he not want to change his thoughts, therefore his life, for the better? I thought I believed in him, in his strength and ability to have what he wanted. I had this path already figured out for him. And I took delight in sharing it with him, too.

However, "changing" yourself was not an appealing notion to Tim. It implied that he was not already comfortable in his own skin, or not liking who he was. The way I presented "change" and "transformation" to him, no matter how excited I was about it, it felt invalidating to his current self. Perhaps, I was too pushy in my approach. And though, it was a magical discovery for me, Tim began to feel that I didn't want to be with him—the one that was—but with some other version of him who was not yet present. Maybe I was so eager to meet and be with his "potential" Self, that I was not validating or supporting the Tim I had. So, he resisted.

Tim has always been a thinker. That I was analyzing and evaluating the way he thought, and critiquing it, was threatening to him. As laid-back as Tim usually was, his message here was extremely firm, as if he were saying, "Hold on Kemila. Growing is good, but hey, I'm already a pretty good person. I don't need to completely change."

While my attempts at "transforming" Tim's mindsets meant that he felt invalidated, similarly, his resistance meant rejection to me. And I was not particularly good at dealing with rejection. All my life, the way I managed rejection was to shut off. Yet rejection still wiggled its way into my awareness through a word, a gesture, a joke, a look, or the lack of a word, a gesture, a joke, a look … There was too much pain in it, old and new, and I protected myself by shutting out the intensity of the pain.

That feeling of being excited about something and wanting to share it with the one I cared for and loved; that enthusiasm was like a colourful helium balloon full of energy, ready to soar. Tim reacted to the way I was presenting it as a threat to Self, so he resisted. And that resistance was like a needle piercing through my bright balloon.

I closed.

He lost.

It was the same patterns, playing out again and again: I would get myself worked up about some new findings about humanity and our thoughts and reality. Then enthusiastically share them with Tim, and Tim not ready to let go of his "old, outdated" ways of thinking, as I was busily presenting my new ideas and logic to him. He would argue, and I would get upset at his "stubbornness". Or worse, I would see him rejecting me as a person, to the point I would yell at him, "Fine, I will never share anything with you again!"

Ironically, I was trying to sell Tim on how thoughts create our reality, shape our beliefs, dictate our emotions and behaviours, and define our happiness. But here I was getting more and more upset about the little things. It got to both of us. Tim wasn't sure if there were underlying issues concerning us that made it happen, or if I was experiencing dissonance between my own true thoughts and what I was reading. He did notice that I was reacting in ways that were at odds with many of the teachings that I had been subscribing to, the things that I had dragged him to watch and listen to, and the ways I had told him I wanted to be.

I remembered how just less than a year before, when we had first met, how he was so praising of me in helping him to think differently, offering him fresh perspectives. I was at a loss with why, suddenly, it had become such a negative thing for him to think differently. Tim tried to provide some insight into this, "Because when we met, you were simply exposing me to new thoughts, not lecturing me like a child."

Somewhere down the road I would hear from someone, "The so-called spiritual people are some of the most judgmental people I know." It was a pitfall. When I finally calmed myself and was completely honest, I knew Tim never had an agenda to change my thoughts and beliefs, he truly viewed them as one's own private responsibility. However, I was so invested in changing his, as if the promised happiness could not be mine if I failed to get his agreement in it.

We were only together for about two months after Tim came back from his long travels. Even though I knew, and I let him know that I knew he was not intentionally trying to agitate or hurt me, I could not help but react. A lot of new hurts surfaced in our interactions during that time, from wounds that only God knew how old they actually were.

One day Tim wrote me an email:

> "My intentions are to treat you with dignity and respect, to be considerate and kind to you and to show you the love that I feel for you. If I am not living up to my intentions, then please, please talk to me about those things. I will do more than my best to improve.
>
> "Otherwise I don't think that my behaviour towards you warrants the way you are treating me. If simply my thinking differently than you is too much for you to bear, then I have no solution for you. I guess that means we're incompatible, and that hurts me tremendously to write. My eyes are filled with tears now. I truly feel that we have some connection that transcends space and time and I have never felt that before. I call that love. But I am almost living in fear

now, never knowing when some innocent thing will upset you and you will turn on me. I love you no matter what you think, and I need you to do the same for me.

"More than anything I want our relationship to grow and deepen and glow with an intensity that bathes us in a nurturing love that allows us both freedoms to grow and to be, in our own ways. Differences can make us stronger.

"I love you Kemila. I loved you before I met you. I will always love you."

Reading the lines from his email, I kept wondering: If for Tim there was no such thing as a "past life", then what did he mean by saying *"we have some connection that transcends space and time"*, and *"I loved you before I met you"*? Nevertheless, something was stronger than all the new hurts and old wounds combined. Neither of us wanted to give up on the other. We openly made that abundantly clear to each other. And that meant, in numerous cases, I had to do things that my poor ego never wanted me to do. What seemed to be a defeat for my ego may have saved our relationship, though. I knew the pattern. Going in another direction, just slightly, could have easily turned this into "just another failed relationship" with an "unwilling man".

Fortunately, it did not play out that way, and I am not sure if I should give credit to all the books I was reading at the time, or if I just knew better. In a way, it was as if I only had one lifetime left to get it right, and I had promised myself that this would be that lifetime, with the loving generosity and support from

Tim—the one who didn't want to make it more difficult, or easier for me; and the one who accepted me as I am, but refused to change himself to please me.

❧   ❧   ❧   ❧

Several years later found me still curious about change. This time, of a greater magnitude, as I realized the ultimate life changing event was death. Out of that great curiosity, I decided to volunteer in a program at the palliative care unit at a hospital near where we lived. It was called the Visiting Program, and I did it for two years, every Sunday afternoon at 2pm. It was my fascination with death that drew me to the program. I wanted to know about death, and always liked to talk about it. But I had no one to talk, or share this interest, with. My mother would always shush me whenever I brought it up as a child. And becoming an adult did not help, either. Nobody seemed to want to engage in a conversation on that kind of subject with me.

On the 10th floor of St. Paul's Hospital, I would visit ward by ward, seeing if there was anything that I could do to help the patients or their families. Most of the time I would simply chat with them. Once I was speaking with a distraught man from Guangzhou, a city in China where I had lived for eleven years, while his sister lay in bed unconscious most of the time. He hadn't seen his sister since she had moved to Canada twenty years before. Now all those years later, he had finally made his way to Canada for a visit, only to find himself in the process of saying a final good-bye to his sister, her body unrecognizable and deformed from cancer.

Sometimes, upon their request, I would play board games or card games with the patients. Once or twice, a patient would play piano or guitar in the common room and I would be their honoured, one and only audience. Other times a patient would delve into philosophical talks with me. One time a 65-year old university professor who had travelled the world, including China many times, rolled over, and pulled off his shirt to show me his back, which was fully covered with beautifully done, stunning tattoos. I felt sad that the art was going to die soon with him. I forget whether I had expressed that sadness with him.

Occasionally patients would candidly talk with me about death, God, and religion. One day, a patient named John asked me with great interest, "So tell me, Kemila, you truly think there is nothing better to do every Sunday afternoon than to watch people die?"

I had to think for a second or two, before I could respond, "No, John. I honestly think there is nothing better for me to do than watch people die on Sunday afternoons."

We had a good laugh together, and then suddenly we shed some tears together.

The next Sunday I went in for my shift. The nurses told me that John had passed away.

11

The Rumpelstiltskin

I continued to occupy myself with a lot of self-paced online courses and read every book on hypnotism that I could get my hands on. Some of those books talked about Future Life Progression, which hugely fascinated, interested, and amazed me.

I have always wondered about the concept of time. I knew that our understanding of time is through man-made measurements. Like any other measuring systems, we created them for the convenience of communication and understanding and interpreting our environment—like grams, ounces, meters, feet (Whose foot is it anyway? I know it's too big to be mine). I do not see these measurements intrinsically existing in our reality. We call it a year when the Earth revolves around the Sun on its obit of a full circle, and we call it a day when the Earth rotates once on its axis. We have agreed upon using the year when supposedly Jesus Christ was born as the beginning of the BCE/CE system. All in all, it is the movement in space that we call time.

If time does not exist except in our own experience with our own creation, it just makes sense to me that we have access to "future" moments the same way that we have access to "past" moments. Both moments are within our mind's reach and creation. I had no idea how much Tim would buy into the idea of Future-Life Progression, and if he didn't, whether it was going to impact our outcome for having another session. But like anything in this physical reality, the only way to find it out was to go there and find out.

One day I proposed to Tim to have another type of "exploring" session to see if we could access a future lifetime. Almost certain there was nothing that could come up, Tim agreed to it, demonstrating his willingness to help. I put on some relaxing music that I always felt was quite futuristic and developed a little hypnosis script to have Tim move swiftly through the vastness of time and space. I told him it would be like travelling on a highway of light, faster and faster through time, beyond this lifetime, to a future moment in time.

Tim proved himself much better at this than he gave himself credit for. To me, this was the most wondrous session.

The opening scene of the session had Tim delighted at having just won a medieval jousting contest. "I managed to knock him off the horse and kill him," he chuckled. Medieval jousting? Had Tim managed to move back in time after all, instead of going forward to a future life?

There was "a group of people watching" the event. And Tim seemed to feel more entertained than satisfied with such a win, even though it sounded a little too savage to me for the beginning of a story. After winning the joust, he said, "we're going for a drink at a cocktail party to laugh about it."

"With your group of people?" I asked. A cocktail party? That did not sound medieval. Maybe he was right after all, by saying that he had an overly active imagination.

"Yeah … Well, everybody."

"What's your name?" I always call the person in front of me by the name of their character in the regression or progression in order to anchor them to that hypnotic trance.

After a long pause, "I don't get anything."

"That's alright. It'll come to you in a moment." This, of course, was a suggestion.

Tim's character eventually explained that he was engaged in an immersive simulation of jousting, something like the virtual reality we have nowadays. And after the competition, he and some good friends, including the one he "knocked off the horse and killed", were going to get together at a cocktail party.

One of the things I usually do at the beginning of a session is have the person go to a place that they call home, "Home can mean a place that you sleep at night." I normally add in case a person does not feel she has a home.

After the cocktail party, I instructed Tim to go "home". There was a silence. I asked, "Are you home?"

"I don't think so." This was an unusual answer. What was going on?

"Where are you?"

"At the ocean. It's quite nice and warm." Tim appeared to be quite relaxed. He described the water spraying upward, catching the sun, and the brilliant blue of the sky.

Maybe his soul identified that nice warm blue ocean as "home". I could not really blame him.

"That was good exercise! I'm stretched out after the swim."

"After the swim, did you come back to the shore?"

"Yeah."

"What are you noticing as you come back to the shore?"

"I'm just going into the beach house. I'll have a shower and dry off."

"Is the beach house yours?"

"Yeah."

"Do you live there alone, or with someone?"

"Alone … more … or less … When I want company, I have company."

"If you want company, who would be there?"

"There are a number of people, depending on …"

"How old are you?" I changed the subject. Suddenly, I wasn't so sure that I wanted Tim to continue with that thought—having several people as his partners?

"A hundred and thirty?" His answer was with a slight rising tone.

I tried not to sound surprised. After all, it should be natural in the future for us to live longer, shouldn't it?

"So, the beach house. Tell me more about it. Like how big it is, what material, what colour it is."

A little pause while focusing, "Well, there's … a long door, glass, and stone. Only one floor, with six or seven rooms."

"Look on the walls of the living room. What's on the wall?"

"Art?" With the same rising tone. I assumed it might be something that was in our future, but in our present reality, the terminology for which had yet to be coined.

"Is there any TV in the living room?" I was going to bring him to a news broadcast to see what was going on in the world and in his local community in that future moment in time.

"No."

"So, you don't watch TV?" What a coincidence! Tim and I don't have a TV set at home, either.

"Things are projected. We don't have dedicated … real estate."

I had no idea what he was talking about. So, I posed the question differently, "So when you want to see what's going on in the news, what do you do?"

"I don't think we have … what you call news. If I have a more specific question, I could ask the house."

An intelligent house! I got even more excited. "Can you ask the house right now the local news?"

"By local, you mean, me? Or people who live with me? Or …"

I reminded myself that I was speaking with someone from the future, I could not take everything for granted. I needed to define things before I used them in questions. And maybe people in the future, having everything at their fingertips, will not need news. "You can ask the house right now, which year this is in."

Tim paused as he inwardly asked the house and interpreted the answer. "Well, I think … it would be about 500 years from now. But this is a different calendar."

"What exact answer did you get?" I did not want the interpretation.

"Two thousand seven hundred forty-one point five seven two." The answer was given robotically.

I imagined the house is like today's smart phones. We were in 2011, so the math would show us over 700 hundred years from now, not 500 years. They must be using a completely different calendar system. What on earth is going on?

"Good. What kind of questions do you normally ask your house?"

"I normally ask for information on things that I am interested in. The house finds the information and summarizes and presents it to me. The house also coordinates transportation for me when I need to go somewhere."

"Ask your house now, what is your name?"

"Sijo." Clearly. Robotically. Unlike the previous attempt to get his name, there was no ounce of doubt or hesitation.

"Sijo, where do you normally go with the transportation coordinated by your house? Do you go somewhere on a daily basis?"

"There is no specific regular routine that I have."

Sounded like Sijo did not need to go to a day job. A good future, I thought to myself. Sijo added, "I do whatever I feel like doing."

"Okay. So Sijo, what are you mostly interested in doing?"

"It's interesting to research things, so perhaps I can contribute a little to human thought. Although, I don't know how much of human thought I can ever know … I play games, and enjoy … entertainments such as the joust, and I take pleasure in the company of friends."

"Where do you normally meet your friends?"

"About half the time we meet at one or the other's residences. And another half of the time, we meet at entertainment complexes for food, drink, or dance … We talk, and tell stories, create, and do things together. We make art together. Create food …"

Sijo was using captivating and distinct choices of words: residence, entertainment complex, create food … I remember when I asked him to "go home", at the beginning of the session, he went directly to the ocean.

"Sijo, when you need to go to your friend's residences, for example, how do you get there?"

"I guess 'flying car' would be the best description."

"So, you just talk to your house, and the house arranges the flying car, and flies it there?"

"Yes ... but the car flies itself, of course."

"Sijo, where you live, it's like a warm island?" The description of the oceanside house sounded quite tropical to me.

"Yes. I live on an island."

"Ask your house, what's the name of this island." I felt lucky. There was this intelligent house which could give me any answers to any questions instantly. I did not need to rely on Tim or Sijo and their memory anymore.

"Rama Ceten."

I was puzzled. "Is it on the Earth?"

"No."

"What's the name of the planet?"

"Patherian." I had never heard of that. And I wondered if I were there too, "I know you have a lot of friends, Sijo, do you have some best friends?"

"Not specifically. The house is very much my closest companion."

"Do you perceive yourself as a male, or do you not have any gender difference?"

"I have been male ... but currently I'm a woman."

"You have been male," I pondered on that statement, "on the same planet, you mean? Or in another life ..."

"We can change genders." Sijo cut me off.

Wow! "So, you have been male. Now you are a woman, in the same lifetime. What are the reasons that you changed?"

"To experience both some time. Some people stay primarily with one gender. I mostly stay as a female. But I am the same person whichever gender I am in."

I wondered what Sijo looked like, "Is there such a thing as a mirror on your planet that you can see yourself with?"

"There are mirrors in the house." Till this day I cannot forgive myself for backing away from further pursuing this question. At the time I was a little afraid that Tim would be freaked out when he looked in the mirror and saw a weird, strange looking being staring back at her. Or, maybe, subconsciously I was afraid that I would freak out?

"Sijo, ask your house what the population is in this year on this planet Patherian."

"The population is currently twenty-eight million four hundred and sixty-three thousand, two hundred and ninety." No blink of the eyes. One breath, robotic.

"Okay," My mind was flooded with so many questions at the same time. Where to start? And I did not want to sound stupid, either.

"Sijo, do you do art from time to time? Like painting? Drawing?" I remembered that Carol had painted.

"I do. But it's difficult to describe … I'm working on a kind of musical sculpture … I don't quite know how better to describe it. The way I create is I kind of visualize the things with the help of the house to create the virtual model, and experience it, like the joust."

"Is it a sort of music that you can see?" I was impressed.

"It's a three-dimensional sculpture that has musical components tied to different batches of elements, and people would be able to interact with, and experience it based on the theme I create."

"How long does it take you to finish it?"

"I think I'll be done within a year."

I asked Sijo to move ahead in time, until a year had passed, to see if the musical sculpture was done.

"I finished it three months ago."

"How was it received?"

"Many people thought it was the fairest expression of joy and sadness that they have ever … seen, I guess that's the word … I think I have achieved what I set out to do."

"Where did you show it?"

"When it was completed, and ready, I coordinated a time when it would become publicly available. And then people could interact with it virtually like I had been doing prior to that. There is no physical thing."

"You mentioned of your sculpture, there was sadness expressed, so people know what sadness is on your planet? Have you yourself ever felt sad?"

"Just because we have physical needs taken care of, we still have emotions, we still love and care for one another, have attractions, fear of rejections. People occasionally leave and come. Departures can be sad."

"For yourself, you are 130 years old now. If you recall, when was the last time you felt sad?"

"10 years or so ago, a person I was with decided to leave." Talking about sadness seemed to have made Sijo sad again,

"They didn't want to be on this planet any longer, weren't sure where they were going, or if they would come back."

I noticed the use of a plural pronoun. Maybe Sijo did not want to apply either he or she.

"Is there any family structure on your planet?"

"People raise kids when they decide to have them. I have had a number over the years."

"You have kids?"

"I had some … about 50 years ago."

"This person who left 10 years ago, had you been together for long?"

"You could say that. But she (I noticed how it had shifted into a singular pronoun now) wanted something else. She wanted to explore."

I moved Sijo forward in time to see if he ever got to see that person again in the future.

After a long pause, "Yes!" It surprised Sijo himself (Sijo really sounded like a male's name to me.) "About 40 or 50 years from now." No kidding. They really live a long life on Patherian.

That person's name was Domac. I took Sijo to the moment of reunion. They realized they were on the same … planet, and that they should say hello. It turned out Sijo had moved to another planet that was called Grandale 7.

"Sijo, how do you travel from Patherian to Grandale 7?"

"By ship?!" Even I felt that was a dumb question to ask.

"Is Grandale 7 in the same solar system?"

"No. It was … I didn't come here directly. I was not sure what the direct travel time would be. I have been to several other places prior to coming here. When I came here, I didn't know that Domac would be here."

"How did you feel, seeing her again?"

"Happy. She's doing well. But it's been a long time. We still get along well, but we realize we are different now. I am not really attracted to her so much anymore."

"So, what's your life like now, Sijo, living on Grandale 7?"

"I'm not sure how long I'll stay. I thought I would just spend several decades travelling. See what that leads me to."

"How do you find Grandale 7?"

"I like the place, but it's different. People do things differently. Where I come from … people tend to live in the tropical areas, because the planet was more or less, an equatorial archipelago. But this planet is more like the Earth where you get large continents, with large forests and more northern kinds of climates. Just little geographic differences seem to change the way that people interact, so I would say that people here seem more reserved and closed... In general, they are slightly larger, slightly bulkier. But maybe the gravity is a little different here too, because I feel a little heavier. I am a male now. Being a male seems to suit me for travel."

"Is it normal for people to travel between planets? Do people need any documentation to travel?"

"No." Hmm, I certainly dream about travelling without visa, passport, or any country borders. An equatorial archipelago sounds like a paradise, or Hawaii. I desperately wanted to know if I were there on the planet as well. I had so many questions! But I was afraid that asking if I, Kemila could be found amongst those Patherians might activate his conscious analytical mind. I would rather him volunteer the information if he could.

117

On that previous island life of Aarn, when I had asked who his young partner Baochi would be in the current life of Tim, he had given the answer, "That could be either you, or Peggy." Peggy was a good friend of Tim's when he was in high school. And in that other life in Canada, Jean LaChance had fought the government and died young. Regretfully, Jean had left a young wife at home. When asked if he had recognition of the wife, Tim had said it was me. Sometimes, I wonder if it was all our wishful thinking.

Sijo continued, "But you have to find a ship going somewhere."

"How big is the ship that you came here with?"

"It was kind of a medium size ship. Just over a million people on it."

"Do you always travel with the same ship?"

"No. Often you just take one ship between places. So that's partially how you decide where to go; just that there is a ship going from where you are to where you are going. Like airports where there are different airplanes going everywhere all the time, there are ships moving from planet to planet. But sometimes, depending on the planet, there may not be any ship going there for several months. But there are planets more central where they may have ships coming and going more than once a day." Go to a train station without a destination. Just catch the next departing train and let it take me wherever it is going. I have done that kind of thing in the past.

Sijo decided to leave Grandale 7 and stay on the ship for a while. It was again a "medium ship" with several-million people on it. The ship itself was an interesting community. Some people lived an extensive part of their lives on it.

"Are there any windows on the ship?" I was wondering what it was like living in space. When I really think about it, aren't we all living in space, even if we are on a planet like Earth? There is only space surrounding us.

"There is nothing that you would call a window, but the ship can project a view anywhere."

That sounded interesting. "Describe to me a view you see."

"If you are traveling between planets, in hyperspace, there is no real view. The ship can create a simulation of … what real space will look like, but there is no … kind of visual perspective or correspondence between hyperspace and real space."

"How's ship life like for you? Do you enjoy it?" To the best of my ability, I imagined it to be like living on a cruise ship.

"I do. There are many people who are very intriguing. And there are very developed games here. I think it will be challenging to master some of those." Sijo then started describing one of the games and its many strategies and tactics before pausing and commenting, "I think I've become a woman again."

"Is there any reason for that?"

"I tend to feel a little more comfortable as a woman."

"I thought you said you feel more comfortable travelling as a man."

"Since I'd like to spend some time here on the ship, I feel more like settling down now."

"How long do you plan to stay on the ship?"

"In total, about 6 or 7 years."

It was getting late. I still had so many questions. Tim came out speaking, "I'm starting to get hungry."

"Okay. We'll end this session soon. Before we do, one last question: Does the ship have a name?"

Sijo answered quickly and clearly, "The Rumpelstiltskin."

I gave Tim/Sijo a suggestion that the next time we did hypnosis, we would come right back to where we left today, on the ship again. Tim nodded his head in agreement, and I was left looking forward to speaking with Sijo again. As life would have it, however, that time has never come. Yet.

Upon wakening from hypnosis, Tim rubbed his eyes and said, "I've certainly read too many science-fiction stories in my younger years!" Maybe you have. But in "science-fiction", where did the authors get ideas from? And why are certain people drawn to science fiction in their younger years and not others?

Obtaining the information in his hypnotic trance was in and of itself a wonder. When Tim did not know my answers to my questions, he simply told me so. Yet when he knew, he seldom hesitated. Some information came clean, clear, and concise. But I also knew that arguing with Tim was useless. I had gotten what I needed.

12

The Story of Me and My Owner

Life had settled itself into a flow. I continued to work my 9 to 5 job, and Tim and I fell into the comfortable pattern of coordinating our nightly dinner and evening plans, at his place or mine, over the phone. Thankfully, we lived close to one another. It was an easy 5-minute car ride or 25-minute walk between our places. I had already met Tim when I had begun looking for a condo to buy, so perhaps subconsciously, I knew I wanted to be nearer to him for future convenience.

In the late spring and early summer of 2008, Tim was planning a road trip back to Saskatoon where he had grown up. The moment he invited me to go with him, I said yes without the slightest hesitation. I had met his parents the previous summer and had enjoyed them immensely. It was Tim, however, who went back and forth about whether it was a good idea or not for me to join him for his family visit. I noticed his discomfort and asked him about it.

"We are Melanchuks," he had replied.

"What is that supposed to mean?"

"That means," Tim looked a little hesitant, "We argue."

Oh fun! I thought.

But Tim was worried about me finding myself in the middle of family disputes.

"Are you worrying about it?" I asked Tim over lunch one day. It was my work lunch hour and we were lunching in Gastown.

"Yup," Tim answered.

"No need to worry about me. I think I can handle it. Every family has its stories; many fight. Sounds like the Melanchuks are simply being a typical family." In the years to come, our own small family between Tim and I would also see its own fair share of fighting.

Road trips always excite me. There was no way I was going to let go of that excitement just because the Melanchuks had disagreements.

We arrived in Saskatoon and were greeted with a heartfelt welcome from Tim's parents and his sister's family. Tim's 10-year old niece was adopted from China, so the family had a little more anticipation than usual to have me there, this Chinese woman who had come to visit and who was becoming a member of the family.

One family dinner while at Tim's parents, his sister, who is usually very observant and can easily see patterns, said something I'll remember forever, "Here we are, seven people at this dinner table. And none of us are blood related." I was very intrigued by that fact, even though I already knew both Tim and his sister were also adopted. Yet not a one of us had a single doubt, that we were indeed a family.

Tim's sister's family planned to take Tim and I on a weekend trip to Waskesiu Lake in Prince Albert National Park, a three-hour drive north of Saskatoon.

I enjoyed the trip immensely. "The Land of Living Skies" was incredible with its vastness, and ever-changing lights and colours. During the drive north in the minivan, accompanied by conversations and the enthusiasm and delight of Tim's niece Natasha, a slightly-Chinese-but-oh-so-Prairie girl, I felt that I fit in with Melanchuks just fine, even in those moments when their voices got raised.

There were many things to do in Waskesiu for the weekend, and Tim's sister had booked us a resort house for our stay. I went with the flow; Tim and his brother in-law set about overseeing the barbecue, and we the ladies went window-shopping. Natasha slipped her little hand into mine as we walked by the lake and through the town. It felt perfect, right, and innocently sweet. But my absolute favourite part of that trip, was when Natasha presented us all with a story she had written, after hearing the story of how her Uncle Tim and Kemila had met:

The Story of Me and My Owner

> Hi, I am Blanket, and I must have made my owner very happy because he found a girlfriend because of me. You bet, it all started one day... It was the day of the Jazz Festival and my owner took me there. Once we were there, he laid me out on the grass and just left me there! He went off. For a while I was just lying there. Then a lady came up to me. She turned and decided to sit on me. I didn't even know her. It took an hour and a half for my owner to come back but he finally returned. He asked the lady what she was doing. She explained to him that she just wanted to

sit on a little corner of his blanket since it was so big. He never even asked me if it was ok! Oh well. Anyway, after a while they started talking and talking and talking and soon, they were laughing. They had a great time together sitting on me. And that is how my owner got a girlfriend. It was all because of me, and it makes me a very proud blanket you know. Because my owner still likes me a lot. I am so happy!

We were all quite amazed at how creative and inspired a 10-year old could be. It was ingenious, really, how Natasha had summed up our story so neatly and accurately all from the perspective of the blanket. I jokingly argued that I hadn't sought the blanket's permission, because it was the blanket itself who had sent out that inviting vibe to me.

This little story made me so happy. It was a very clever and playful way of letting me know that Tim's family had fully accepted me into the family.

To this day, Tim and I still use that blanket for summer outdoor activities. We do not have any intention of retiring it. Nor, do we feel like framing it on the wall. The romantic story was told and captured. But life goes on.

13

Are There Fish in Your Ocean?

It had been almost a full year since Tim and I had first started exploring past and future lives. The journey had been extremely satisfying, exciting, and rewarding for me. During that time, I had graduated from the Hypnotherapy school, left my full-time job, and enrolled myself into a self-employment program to start my own practice.

I continued practicing with Tim. Everything I learned, I first tried with him: Parts Therapy, Ultra Hypnosis, Timeline Regression Therapy, Pain Management, Weight Loss, Dynamic Imagery, Core Transformation …

For some of those techniques Tim just went along with me. With Ultra Hypnosis, I tested his depth by suggesting he forget the number between 6 and 8 when counting, just like in stage hypnosis shows. It worked brilliantly. Some of the other methods we utilized for better sleep and weight release.

Even though I had officially graduated from the Hypnotherapy school, and had received my diploma, I found that there was still so much to learn.

In those early weeks of my new career, I did not have many clients. I did have, however, plenty of time on hand in which to study and experiment. One day, I put Tim into a trance and invited his higher wisdom to come through. I didn't exactly have a clear vision of what I was doing, but I decided to experiment on the idea of accessing "deeper wisdom" through a hypnotic state. As Tim's breathing slowed, and his muscles softened, I instructed him to open his inner doorway leading to his "Inner Advisor". Later, I would dub it TIA – Tim's Inner Advisor.

The same voice as Tim's spoke, but it was tempered with a calmer and more confident tone. With an unspeakable excitement in my own subconscious mind, I went ahead and presented the challenges of my new career, and asked for directions, steps, marketing, and structuring guidance. TIA answered all my questions and gave me extremely useful information about things I could start doing. To keep the objectivity of what flowed through the session, we both referred to me in the third person as 'Kemila'. On a Soul level, TIA connected my business with my own character. It became very meaningful to me. Very soon, I had found that I had taken four full pages of session notes.

TIA really got me, understood me quite deeply, and unlike Tim, spoke my language. Significant as the messages were on many levels, they were also very practical. Soon after the session, I found myself implementing those very same ideas and steadily started moving forward in my new enterprise.

Unfortunately, not all my efforts went as brilliantly as TIA. I had been completely astonished, overjoyed and elated even, with how well the Future Life Progression to the life of Sijo had gone. But my super-enthused-self did not make sense to Tim. For him, tired and hungry as he was when we finished some of those sessions, it was like, *"You put me in a relaxed trance state and asked me some questions. I gave you some answers that easily came to my awareness. It was pretty easy for me to do. What's the big deal of it?"*

Perhaps there was no virtue in what came easily; things with real value had to come through struggle and challenge. Maybe my enthusiasm was indeed overly done. But it did not seem overdone to me. It was simply the right amount of expression of my rather real excitement. Obsessed with obsessions. We are, after all, all the same, just different subjects.

It was easy for me to find both the Sijo and Carol characters in Tim. You may call me a dreamer, but I live with a thinker who possesses very refined artistic tastes. In both Carol and Sijo, as well as Tim, I could see how much this soul genuinely enjoys ruminating and intellectualizing. Traits I try not to identify with myself.

I was exceedingly grateful to Tim for opening my mind and expanding my horizons via hypnosis. He managed to answer so many of my questions as Sijo. Yet, I found myself left with more questions than answers: What is the average life span on Patherian? Are there fish in the ocean? And dolphins? What animals are on Patherian? What is the food like? What is people's understanding and practice of spirituality like there? Do Patherians have health issues? Or, is everyone always healthy? Is the soul currently known as Kemila there on Patherian?...

Once again, my enthusiasm only added more pressure on Tim. What started out as an easy exploration, soon became laden with my excitement and subconscious agendas. When my nephew came to visit, I found myself telling this story to him without first consulting Tim. Perhaps, it was just another way of me seeking my nephew's admiration. But at that time, Tim was still hesitant to share these experiences with anyone other than myself.

I had also talked about blogging about Sijo's story, maybe even turning it into a movie. I felt electrified and talked about a great many things. One day I was reading a psychology research paper. It mentioned that for children, too much praise for an activity they have been otherwise enjoying for its own sake, such as sports, drawing, writing, or singing, can make them lose interest in it altogether. This discovery seemed not only applicable to children, but obviously I thought, to an adult Tim, as well.

Tim knew about my fascination with several people who channelled other beings, had become famous, and developed significant followings as spiritual teachers. I compared Tim with these spiritual celebrities. That was my bigger mistake than all the praise I had showered him with. Tim passionately did not want to become "some kind of guru".

So, to my great disbelief, revisiting the life of Sijo never happened. Presumably, Tim did not see the point, yet I ran out of ways to make him see it. My tactics in this matter simply no longer worked; my ambition had outgrown Tim's interest. It was too late.

Tim saw my struggle. He wanted to help, but my earnestness had grown too much for him to continue to be comfortable. After all, the material that came out of the regression and progression sessions, although making perfect sense to me, were to him simply, "fabrications of his unconscious imagination". I was reading too much into and making too much of a big deal out of his own vivid imaginings.

Midnight, on a cold Thursday in November. Tim was in bed, sound asleep. I put on my shoes and a thick down-filled jacket, locked the door, and went to Stanley Park for a walk. My feet took me to Second Beach where the ocean waves are forever gentle. I lay my body down on a lone big log and looked up at the clear night sky. In that moment the sky opened up before me and millions of stars twinkled back at me, expressive, yet silent, moving through space, yet still to my eyes. I said to myself: Surrender. There is truly nothing I need to be attached to, nor fight against. Stories can be told many different ways. They found me now. And here I was.

My body became as cold as the night itself, telling me it was time to go home. I got to my feet, and not even once looking back to the stars in the sky, I went home.

14

A Spy in the Sky

Two months had passed since that future life progression as Sijo. And I had finally come to terms with the fact, that this type of work truly could not be rushed or forced. It was Tim's mind that was all I had to work with, the same mind from which willingness would come, as much as regression or progression information. Even though Hypnotists divide it into the conscious and unconscious minds, there is only one mind through which information flows. Or not. The point I myself had failed to see was that too high an expectation had scared Tim.

When my birthday came up again, I requested Tim to have another session with me as another birthday gift. To let him feel less pressured, I suggested, "We don't have to go back to Sijo's life. We can simply do a general exploration towards the future. Wherever we land would be fine." Tim agreed.

Having said that, during the hypnosis induction, I asked Tim to go through a tunnel of time to a future moment, to a scene that "your subconscious mind is actually quite familiar with, either on your own planet, a planet that you visited, or on a spaceship, that will be easy and natural and normal for you." After this rapid induction, and as a trance deepening technique, to make it even more Sijo-life related, I ingeniously started by having Tim, in his mind's eye, gaze into a starry night sky. In the background, I played the same futuristic, relaxing music as before.

Knowing Tim might still be a little nervous about "performing", I had a back-up plan. I would guide him down to a beach for further deepening, and hopefully that would link to Sijo's beach house. Worst case scenario, I would end up using the beach imagery to guide him into a deep hypnotic, relaxed state and then give him suggestions to prepare his unconscious mind for a future re-visit of the memories.

This time, Tim's mind does not work with my covert agenda. His subconscious mind takes everything literally, and he goes to a future lifetime on a different planet called Paradigm! The year is 423 of the Green Era which followed the Whisper Era.

"Take a few moments now to allow everything to come into crystal clear focus; information is flowing into your awareness, and the scene is becoming visible. Let yourself be reoriented to this new environment; focus on it. And when you allow it to come into crystal clarity, more information will flow into your awareness. What do you see?"

He was in bed, and just waking up. In this life he was called Saren.

"How do you feel? Do you feel warm or cool? Or anything else?"

"I feel … perfect." The word 'perfect' was stressed with a perfectly satisfied tone.

Soon Saren's room began growing lighter, one of the walls turned transparent providing a breathtaking view of a pristine mountain valley with a turquoise lake nestled at the bottom. Saren's bed gently lowered onto the surface below before completely releasing him. He got up and wrapped himself in a soft silver-blue robe. Listening to Saren talk **reminded me of Tim, someone with high standards and an appreciation of the finer things in life.**

After having a morning espresso, automatically provided by the house, Saren dressed for the day and left.

"Something is on your agenda today?"

"Yes. I'm going into a city to meet with other people."

The questions and answers were simple, but the process was more like Tim watching a movie and then explaining the movie to me simultaneously. I needed to time my questions exactly right. There were instances, after a long pause, when Tim was just about to answer a previous question, but I had already jumped on to the next question before he could answer. Working with Tim was trying my patience, of which I do not have much.

The house arranged a personal flying vehicle to ferry Saren to the home of Rotan, where he was meeting with Rotan and four others, only two of whom would be physically present. They were there to discuss an alien civilization called the Fahaer who occupied an area of the galaxy near the space used by Saren's civilization.

"The Fahaer, are they friendly or not?"

"They are neither friendly nor hostile. It's more potentially bothersome."

"In terms of …?"

"They have different values from us. And although we are not currently acrimonious, we foresee that our values conflict. They are a more … how you would say, hierarchical, or aggressive type of society or civilization, which we anticipate will eventually become hostile towards us."

Saren's civilization by contrast was a loose federation of different human groups who had been coexisting peacefully with each other for centuries. The Fahaer were a relatively new development, and Saren was a spy posing as a diplomat working with the others to find a non-military option of neutralizing the threat posed by the Fahaer.

The meeting concluded. Saren was reluctant to share with me any of the plans or conclusions that his group had determined. I presumed being a spy, Saren was professionally trained not to reveal things quite so easily, even in a hypnotic state!

I did, though, get him to divulge some simple background information about himself and his civilization. Saren was born on a planet named Eleanor where he had spent his first six years. His parents were a little itinerant and kept moving the family about. Saren attributed his upbringing as to why he himself kept moving.

"I spend time on what you would call far flung places, places that are on the edges of our civilization; places that others don't go or that involve a long ships travel." I imagined how exotic that would be. "… Gaining a first-hand perspective is how I contribute to my society."

As a spy, understandably, Saren did not have close connections with people or places. Travel and change were essentially what he knew. And had always known.

"Are you saying you do not have friends?"

"I have friends, or people I get along with better than others. But I don't appear to hang out with people who may have questions."

Seemed like a necessary quality, or a wise strategy for a covert operative.

The session had lasted for over two hours. Tim tried to move his body around; he had grown uncomfortable lying unmoving on the couch. He asked for a drink of water. And with that, he brought himself out of the trance, and back to the present day, back to Earth.

15

Onto the Promised Path

It's interesting how in our daily existence one thing can lead to another, which leads to another, and leads to another, without one knowing what is going to happen before it occurs; everything converges together, to make the most unusual possible.

Such as me becoming a Hypnotherapist.

A lot of people, mostly my clients, have asked me this question: How did you choose this profession?

Some things you choose. Other things choose you.

It may sound like a cliché, but sometimes that really is how life unfolds. I feel that I did not choose the profession, at least, not consciously. I would not have believed you, all those many years ago, if you had told me that I would become a Hypnotherapist, not until I had already become one. Hypnotherapy chose me.

To explain how that happened, I usually go for the short version, which says, "A chain of events happened, and I took one step, and then another. Before I knew where each step was leading me, I became a Hypnotherapist."

Occasionally, when time or relevance allows, I share the longer version of the same story:

There was a moment in my childhood—back in China—that I have never forgotten. I was reading a big book or a magazine, in which there was a drawing of a man standing by what was possibly a recliner; another man was reclining on it. There may have been others in the background, like an audience or some assistants. I cannot remember the details. Both men looked like people from the 18th or 19th century in the West. The caption read that the standing man was hypnotizing the seated man.

Consciously, I was quite likely thinking that it was a man helping another to sleep better. In my youth, that was as much as I could fathom about hypnotism.

Yet unconsciously, I felt an unusual level of excitement. Nothing was truly peculiar about the book or magazine, or even the scientific representation of the drawing. It was all in that word, *'hypnotizing'*. In that ordinary moment, with that singular word combined with that very ordinary drawing, I found myself hypnotized into an ecstatic state.

Many years later I would move to Canada, I was in my mid-thirties then. I had no idea what my life was going to become. The purpose of emigrating was simply to become a Canadian, so that I could freely travel the world with a Canadian passport—more than 170 countries without a need for a visa! To do that though, I first had to focus on the practical aspect of making a living. I had a fear that I could not make it—that I would not have enough money to live on. I jumped into the first job that I could find, one paying minimum wage.

One evening, while reading a business magazine that had been recycled by the woman from whom I rented a small basement suite, I found an article which discussed the salary scales in different professions. It said a counsellor could earn 90 to 110 dollars an hour. I was shocked, delighted, and resentful, all at the same time. That was a lot of money, just for talking with someone!

I wanted this. Didn't I? Yet some voice in me uttered loudly, *"But who are you to want that?"*

Of course, it wasn't meant for me, was it?

It was not just the earning potential of that profession that attracted me and got me thinking; the article was about salary scales for many different professions. There were other professions that could also earn that much money and even more. But my attention was obsessively drawn to counselling and psychology. Regardless of that discouraging loud voice inside me, or the fact that I had no training in either counselling or psychology, I still wanted it. It was a nudging, niggling feeling deep from within.

Many more years passed. I finally started working at a job that paid better, that I enjoyed. I felt as if I had "arrived". I worked an administrative position at an investment company. The company's location was superb! Right in Harbour Centre in downtown Vancouver, with a view overlooking the harbour and North Shore mountains. The company was a private investment club, we accepted memberships; and my job lay in security filing. I became adept at it and my observational skills, sensitivity, and logical reasoning, seemed to be a great fit.

There were times when I would read a member's date of application, and then relay to my Membership Service colleagues the details of which the member had joined: at which event they'd joined; what had happened when they'd joined; and other things that had been going on at the time of them signing up, including the occasional membership fees that had been overlooked, and therefore, not charged. My colleagues were amazed by my effortless recall and asked how I knew all these things. In turn, I was shocked by their surprise. To me everything was obvious, the application forms were crystal clear, no analysis or interpretation needed. I was simply reading the same papers as they were, in plain English, which was their first language not mine.

"How do you know everything?" They would ask me.

"How did you *not* know?" I would answer back.

Soon, the office started calling me, "Detective Kemila". It baffled me, even though I happily accepted the title.

It was during my time at the investment company that I met Tim, in the summer of 2007.

In 2008, after Tim had finished his part of the documentary, he was left with a professional video camera, microphones, and other odds and ends of the trade. As some of the self-help books I was reading would encourage readers to dream big, I started to dream about becoming a documentary film producer. I knew I did not possess the relevant training, skills, or experience. Then again, if I were experienced it would not be "dreaming big", would it? I wrote affirmations and said to myself everyday:

I am a successful filmmaker.
I make successful documentaries.
I am a successful film producer.

What to produce, though? I had no idea, but I did have a cameraman with a big professional camera.

I thought, first I would need to find a project for a good cause. Next, I would apply for government grants. The action steps seemed straightforward. And weren't they?

One day I heard about a local "healer" who was going to take a group of people to Egypt—*Multidimensional Journey through Egypt* as they called it. What does it mean to be on a multidimensional journey? I had no idea, but it sounded interesting to me. And "Healer" was a strange sounding word to my ears. I thought about doctors, and knew it was more than that. How much more? Again, I did not have the slightest clue.

But Egypt! Now, that I could handle. I wrote a proposal to whomever would fund my documentary, using the information I had read up on:

> "The crew of two will follow a healer, author, artist and spiritual teacher to Egypt; an ancient place well-known for its healing ability, where he will explore healing using sacred geometry, meditation in a sacred space, and other healing practices and spiritual discovery with a group of seekers from Canada. Picturesque and thought provoking, this documentary will lead viewers to ponder on questions such as transition and transformation of life, and spiritual development. We believe by making this documentary we are being of service and bringing deeper value to humanity."

The dream of being a film producer was grand and exciting. Unfortunately, the dream did not last long. As the rejections rolled in, we lost the opportunity to go on that tour. As quickly as the dream had been born, it expired.

Something else did not seem to want to fade with it, though. One day during my office lunch break, I went for a walk a few blocks away to Cathedral Square and enjoyed my lunch in the sun for a half hour. As I was walking down Richards Street on my way back to the office, I heard a voice—but there was no one around me. There was a woman walking beside me but she was paying me no mind. And, it was not even a woman's voice that I had heard. It was a male-sounding voice, and the voice was coming from inside my own head. It said, *"But YOU are a healer."*

It felt strange to me that the sentence started with the word "but"; although I immediately knew it was referring to the fact that I was trying so hard to film a healer.

"No. That's mistaken," I tried to correct it. "I was wanting to become a film producer. I was going to film a healer. And I have failed."

"But YOU are a healer." That voice did not argue. Its tone did not change. It simply repeated itself with the same emphasis as before.

"I am *not* a healer. I have no medical or even science degree. I can potentially be anything but that!" I was annoyed, and strangely scared.

"But YOU are a healer." The voice had nothing more to offer me except for that one perplexing statement.

"You have got to be kidding!" I thought to myself. I brushed it off and stepped into the elevator in my office building.

※ ※ ※ ※

After our first road trip from Vancouver to Saskatoon in June 2008, Tim, my nephew Devin, and I, were crazy enough to drive through the icy, snowy, Rocky Mountains and Prairies again. This time heading back to Saskatoon for Christmas. In good weather, it is a trip that takes two long, full days of driving in either direction. We were on the second leg of the drive back home through B.C.'s Thompson Okanagan region when the sky began to darken. Much to Tim's chagrin, I was dozing off in the passenger's seat, as I am apt to do on long drives. But outside on the treacherous Coquihalla Pass it was snowing. In my half-wake, half-sleep state, I heard Tim say, "Talk to me. Say something. This snow is coming right at me. The way it is being lit up by the headlights in the dark, I feel like I'm being hypnotized."

"Hypnotized!" I was instantly wide-awake upon hearing that word. "What did you just say?"

I loved the sound of it. The word was full of electricity to me. I sat up, looked at Tim, and asked, "Can you say it again?"

No fear, no annoyance, just an all-encompassing excitement with that word, with that energy. It was a magnetic kind of attraction that I did not wish to brush off, either.

❦ ❦ ❦ ❦

Every year, my employer held a conference called *InvestFest*, consisting of many speakers over the course of a weekend. There were talks chock full of investment strategies and portfolios, charts, and numbers; needless to say, the conference could get quite boring. In the spring of 2009, after a long first day of the conference, the company had invited a hypnotist from Las Vegas to conduct a live stage show as some much-needed entertainment.

This was the speaker I had been dying to hear since the list of speakers had been announced. I had continued reading my

143

self-help books and was beginning to form a clearer understanding of the power of the subconscious mind, and I was counting down the hours until the hypnotist show. As with most of the conference's other speakers, there was an upsell: A weekend seminar he called, *The Turning Point*. I was at a turning point in my own life, and I was ready to transform, to turn my life around. However, there was a setback, the weekend seminar would cost me three thousand and eight hundred dollars.

But I was not going to give up that easily, not on a seminar I so badly wanted, *needed* to take part in, just because of a large price tag. Yet, I hesitated and waited until the last possible minute to sign up. The seminar was to take place at the end of summer, so I still had months to go before I needed to commit.

✤ ✤ ✤ ✤

I kept up with my self-expansion through self-help books, and the deadline for signing-up for *The Turning Point* approached. One day, on one of my many visits to the Vancouver Central Library, I walked down the aisle of the Social Science section, slowly browsing the bookshelves. Suddenly, one book fell off the shelf, as if by its own volition, and landed smack in front of me. I picked it up, intending to re-shelve it. Then I thought it would be better to place it on the sorting tray at the end of the aisle, leaving it to a librarian to properly shelve. While walking the book over to the tray, I looked at its dark cover, *Journey of the Souls* by Dr. Michael Newton. I had never heard of the book, nor its author. As if it were speaking to me, something on the book's cover drew my attention. After a second thought, I decided to put *Journey of the*

Souls in my basket and check it out. If I didn't like it, I could easily return it to the library.

Life was never the same for me after that.

My nights were utterly and completely consumed. Every night I could not wait to get to bed and read that book. With each page I turned, I could hardly believe what I was reading. A whole new world, yet one so familiar, was opening up, beckoning me in and bringing me closer to its truth. It was wild, yet so real. I read and gasped. This couldn't be true, yet nothing else was truer than that.

Dr. Michael Newton used hypnotherapy to regress individuals back to their pure spirit state. He called this state, *Life-Between-Lives*. It was beyond past lives. And here I was, barely introduced to the idea of past lives!

The discoveries haunted me. I spent days wondering what to do with them.

I craved that experience!

Whilst researching the author, Dr. Michael Newton, it led me to the Newton Institute website. There, I found a local hypnotherapist and booked my first hypnotherapy session with her.

In our email exchanges, the hypnotherapist told me that we would first have a past life experience, since I had never done hypnotherapy before.

I shared with Tim that I had made a hypnotherapy appointment for a past life regression. Tim had no idea what to make of it. "Okay" was all the response I was to get.

Prior to arriving at the appointment, I decided to make a list. High on the list was whether I had met Tim before in another lifetime. I must have treated hypnotherapy like magic—as many of my later clients would do. Soon I had listed all my big and small problems, including, why I felt an aversion to a colleague in my office; what the ringing tone in my right ear was about; what were my roles in my previous relationships, and on and on the list went.

Even with the host of things I had on my list, I did not consider booking more than one hypnotherapy session. However, my hypnotherapist suggested, "Since you've never had this kind of experience before, and you have this tinnitus in your ear, today we'll mostly work to condition your mind, and we'll work on the tinnitus. I'll record the session and send it to you. You'll listen to the recording for a week, so then when you come back, we can have a past life regression."

She then went ahead and established a "control room" in my subconscious mind. I could go inside the control room, find the dial, and dial down the ringing sound in my ear. It didn't work. I was not even sure if I wanted to eliminate the ringing sound in my right ear yet. I just wanted to find out more about it. The hypnotherapist had taken it for granted and presumed that I wanted to rid myself of the ringing.

Earlier I had read in one of Doreen Virtue's books that tinnitus might be an indication of souls coming from other stars. That I might have a connection with another star system was naturally a very thrilling thought to me; many times, Earth societies and human interactions can feel quite alien to me. As annoying as it was at times, I was not completely sure if I wanted to mute the ringing sound just yet.

During the session, the hypnotherapist guided me to a beautiful relaxing place, I went to an imagined scene in Greece. Suddenly, my nose started itching. Seeing how I was supposed to be hypnotized, I thought I wasn't meant to move my hand and scratch it. Thinking that, if I performed such a conscious act, I would have somehow failed the hypnotherapist. My need to perform for her outweighed my need to do a basic, natural, usually subconscious, act of scratching an itch. And so, the rest of the session became quite excruciating. The longer she continued to try and relax me, the deeper my suffering became. All I could do, while in a "trance", was focus on when the hypnotherapist would finish the session, so that I could scratch my nose.

Consequently, as I was walking out of her office, I did not feel a sense of having been hypnotized. *"Maybe I can't be hypnotized"*, I rationalized to myself. *"After all, I am a very strong-willed person."*

I did not book another session with her. However, something else worked. In our earlier email exchanges, when I had asked the hypnotherapist about her background, she had said she used to be a musician, and that English was also her second language. For some reason, I had found those two facts very encouraging. In that initial moment when I'd first arrived at her office, there had also been a clear and concise voice inside me saying, *"You can do this!"*

❦   ❦   ❦   ❦

I was satisfied with my job, where people respectfully called me Detective Kemila. I was not looking for any new work opportunities, yet my mind kept drawing me back to the idea of doing hypnosis.

Two months after my first ever hypnotherapy session, I was reading a free natural health and wellness magazine, and a little four by two-inch advertisement caught my eye. It read:

Become A Certified Clinical Hypnotherapist

Learn to Use Your Own Mind Power and Help Others Reach their Goals

Earn your certification as a Clinical Hypnotherapist on weekends allowing you to continue working while training for an exciting career

Accepting Applications Now!

Call for your FREE Course Catalogue

A toll-free phone number was listed at the bottom. I picked up my phone and called.

After speaking for about a half hour with Brick Saunderson, whose voice was kind and mesmerizing, I was thoroughly convinced to sign up with his hypnotherapy training school. Brick said he would mail out more information for me to read before I fully committed to enrolling in the course. But I knew I was already sold. The tipping point was that the tuition for the entire year of the part-time certification course would be three-thousand and eight-hundred dollars, plus book and registration fees.

Three thousand and eight hundred dollars! I had already been prepared to spend on a weekend seminar where someone would teach me how to harness my subconscious mind. Wouldn't it be an even greater bargain if I could learn how to do that myself and become certified to practice it?

I put down the phone, still excited. Tim was sitting in the same room but was completely absorbed by his computer monitor. He knew I was on the phone with someone, but he simply had not been paying active attention to my conversation with Brick. Breathlessly, I filled him in, "I just signed up for a hypnotherapy certification program."

"What?!" Tim looked up at me, surprised by what he had heard.

I thought to myself, *"Yeah. What, did I just do?"*

16

Like Becoming a Butterfly

Eight more months had passed since the life as Sijo. I decided to give it another try by simply asking Tim if he would have another hypnosis session with me. He said, "Yes".

I used the same favourite induction to float Tim's awareness out of his body, lifting him up, rising higher and higher, all the way through the Earth's atmosphere, into the centre of the universe. Then gently, as I counted from 20 to 1, I asked Tim to continue to float and find "another planet" to land on.

Since I had my own agenda for the session, I inserted some suggestions into my backward counting, "You know, anything can happen in your creativity and imagination and memories. When we say memories, we include memories of the future. The wonder of hypnosis is that we have access easily, naturally, effortlessly, to all these memories. No time, no space, is any barrier to that. It doesn't matter if it is about a location of, say, an island such as *Rama Ceten*. Or, a moving spaceship such as the *Rumpelstiltskin*. I don't know if it's easy for you to access … Maybe through an intelligent beachside house … Maybe just a general impression on a planet such as *Patherian*, or *Grandale 7*? All I know is that you are eager to take on this journey, to discover and explore ... 3, 2, 1 ... Touching the ground now. Quickly, day or night?"

"Day."

"Indoors or outdoors?"

"Outdoors."

"Alone or with someone?"

"Alone."

"Look around. See where you are. What surroundings do you find yourself in?"

There's confusion, and silence.

I shifted his attention back to the body, "Look at your feet, what are you wearing on your feet?"

"I'm pretty much naked."

Huh? Daytime, outdoors, alone, naked?!

Tim started to describe his surroundings, "It's barren, like a desert; dusty, very windy."

"Are you male or female?"

"Male."

"What are you thinking, and what are you feeling, in this moment?"

"I'm a little puzzled by this environment. I'm not sure what's going on." The personality was just as confused as the hypnotist.

"Do you have any sensation in your body while you are there?"

"No."

"Nothing else is going on?"

"No."

"Okay. You are there by yourself. You don't know much of what's going on, but you do know your name. Spell your name to me."

"R-A-M-R-U-T".

I was a little disappointed. Again, it was not Sijo after all.

What a hypnotist can do, is to give suggestions. Sometimes it works, sometimes it doesn't. When a mind does not want to take in a suggestion, for any variety of reasons, it will reject the suggestion. Hypnosis is not mind control as is commonly misunderstood. I often tell my new clients my simplistic definition of hypnosis. It is only composed of two words— *Suggestions accepted*.

A hypnotist can only give suggestions. Like on a stage show, a hypnotist would give suggestions in a tone that normally sounds like a command. When the suggestion is accepted by willing participants, (because they have volunteered onto the stage), the participants act on that suggestion. It gives the audience the impression that when the hypnotist commands, the participant follows, then "It must be mind control."

For some reason, maybe Tim really was done with Sijo's story. My covert suggestions during the induction did not work. I had to let it go and be grateful that at least he was not done with Carol's life. Yet.

Still I was fascinated. I wondered how Ramrut had come to land naked in the middle of that stark and desolate backdrop. "Okay. Ramrut, how do you travel?"

"I walk. Or I take different kinds of transport, depending on where I'm travelling to."

But you said nothing was there. I had to remind myself to stay open-minded, even though the more answers I got, the more confused I became. "Describe an example of a transport."

"Spaceships. Hyper-fast, sub-surface transport. Flying cars." Instead of one example, Ramrut gave me three.

Indeed, this might be another alien life!

"Ramrut, I'm going to give you a keyword. This keyword is 'home'. That is where you sleep at night. When I count from 3 to 1, you will be there. 3, 2, 1, you are there now! Where do you find yourself?"

He went to a vastly different environment, with a large living space, opening onto a garden. There were tables and chairs in the living space, and melancholic, abstract, yet colourful surrealistic art on the walls.

I asked Ramrut, "You were almost naked in a barren land, to now this living space. How exactly did you get from there to here?"

He replied, "I think about it."

I took a deep breath. It's that simple, huh? Especially for a thinker like this one.

That is part of the reason I love what I do. I can always expect the unexpected.

It turned out that the preliminary scene was like the simulation jousting game at the beginning of Sijo's session. But instead of using a computer-generated scene, this scene was real; Ramrut's consciousness was essentially projected into another body.

Since Ramrut could think himself into different places or bodies, he might just think himself into any answers to my questions, "Now, I want you to think about it, and you'll know the answer: Which year is this?"

"Relatively, at least 1000 years more than where your time is now."

"Now think about it, what's the name of your planet?"

That proved to be a question based on an assumption. Ramrut was not on a planet, but in an artificial world that formed a ring around a star. Over two hundred billion people lived on that ring that they called Plaquan. Somehow though, there was still day and night. People did not need to sleep but most people choose to, including Ramrut.

"Do you live by yourself?"

Ramrut lived as a part of an intimate group with three women. I did not quite know how to think about that. Groups, of varying sizes, seemed to be the organizing units of society rather than pairs as we have now. And groups seemed more fluid than conventional marriages. They fluctuated over time, and on a regular basis. Sometimes several groups would come together and decide to form a larger group. And sometimes groups didn't even live together, but still shared communication and emotional bonds.

"What do you normally do?"

"I explore. I create. I indulge. Many of them overlap."
Ramrut sounded just like Carol, or Tim, or Sijo.

"When you create, what do you create?"

"I create music with a sort of visual aesthetic that goes with the music. I try to create in terms of knowledge. I try to advance through knowledge of the world, or the universe perhaps, through science and art."

Visual music. It reminded me of Sijo again.

"How do you normally communicate with each other?"

"We form thoughts. We don't need to talk verbally. It's easy to communicate through thoughts, but even then, we are still using language."

"Like telepathic communication?"

"Like directly thinking to each other. Bonding with a group opens our minds and bodies at an intimate level."

"You said sleeping is optional. What about food, do people eat?"

"That is part of the indulgence. It's fun to play and create and eat."

"And drink?"

"All kinds of intoxicating substances!" Ramrut spoke with a tone of pleasure. It again reminded me of Carol, or Tim. As they say, many lives, the same inclinations.

"What kind of food do you eat? For example, do you eat plants, or meat?"

"We don't kill animals, but we certainly have proteins or other substances, almost identical to animal flesh. We have a greater variety of things to play with because essentially everything is manufactured. So that allows a greater variety of different flavours, textures, and colours than would occur naturally. We look at some of the underlying chemistry and its relationship with how our senses work, to create the foods that we eat, much like how we compose music."

I started to feel this might be Tim's way to perceive a life-between-lives state. Even Dr. Michael Newton had said that souls in the in-between state, do all sorts of things, and engage in all sorts of activities, studies, and creations. Without a conscious acknowledgement to himself of the existence of an in-between-lives state, the only way Tim's mind could translate what he perceived in the hypnotic trance was that it was a virtual reality on the artificial ring with artistically manufactured foods, even though there was a perceived body.

"What is people's understanding of spirituality on Plaquan?"

"We don't have religion but that sense of connectedness and transcendence which spirituality brings is associated with groups in our society." Didn't Dr. Newton call it "soul clusters", "soul groups", or "soul families"?

Ramrut explained further, "Groups can be much deeper than simply emotional and sexual connections. They also help people grow and learn. When people join groups, such as ours, there will be a level of spiritual experience there. For those who want an even deeper experience, they can choose to join a permanent 'group mind', where they leave the physical realm behind. There are various types and sizes of group minds, focusing on different kinds of empathic, intellectual, creative, or emotional experiences. We can literally share with each other what we experience. Group minds in our society can become particularly large and complex, almost mystical."

Putting what Ramrut said into the context about a pure spiritual state, with physical reality a projection of that, I felt I could follow more than thinking it was another advanced future lifetime. I reminded myself that when I was speaking with an otherworldly intelligence, I first needed to lay down any preconceived notions and concepts I might have.

"How do you travel in your Ring?"

"Depending on how far, I use something like a subway but more personal and much, much faster."

"Where you live, is it like a city, or a suburb?"

"It's closer to a city. We don't really have suburbs so much. Suburbs are a result of a combination of scarcity and abundance. We don't really have scarcity."

"What do people look like? Just like humans? Or different?"

"More or less like humans, but we have in some degree much greater variation."

"Describe the variations."

"One thing, the skin colour. Our skin can be almost any colour, by choice. We can also change skin colour."

"Have you changed your skin colour before, Ramrut?"

"I'm not a fashion person, so I have a standard gold brown skin colour. Slight, but not a significant variation."

"For people who are into fashion, what kind of skin colours could they have?"

"Whatever is in the rainbow," he replied in a sing-song voice.

I quickly entertained the idea of rainbow coloured skins walking around a city. And for some reason I was quite confident that there was no racism on Plaquan. "Okay, that's skin colour. Tell me more about other variations."

"Well ... some people choose to have tails. There are people almost completely covered with hair. And in extreme cases, it could be having feathers, or scales, or almost anything that can be, depending upon the environment in which they choose to live in. But most people maintain a basic humanoid type of appearance when living in a standard environment."

"That means whatever you choose ... You don't necessarily walk on all fours?"

"No. Our society draws on the basic archetype. Other societies, I guess, could be different. They could choose a different standard body type. That's different kinds of races, though."

"When you say other societies, or races, do you mean different Rings? Or the same Ring?"

"Different. Other Rings, planets, or spaceships, other groups of people."

"From where you are now, are you aware of the planet that is called Earth?"

"Yes."

"Do you have any knowledge about it?"

"Well, that's where humans originated."

"So, is it from there that they made this Ring?"

"Not *from* there, but eventually, or indirectly."

"From where you are, are you able to travel to Earth?"

"Yes. Basically, it's preserved as a park, or a shrine now."

"But it's not a residential place anymore?" I was not sure how the Earth could host several hundred billion people.

"No."

I already loved travelling all over the world so much; I imagined what it would be like for the Earth to become a planet-wide system of natural, semi-natural and developed conservation areas of human significance.

"So, in your lifetime, Ramrut, have you been to Earth?"

"No."

"Speaking of lifetimes, what is the life span on the Ring?"

"Well, somewhat indefinite. Eventually most people choose to 'fuse' with a group. But it's possible to keep one's physical body working well for … hundreds of years."

"Is time travel a reality there?"

"That is still part of the exploration. Science and art in many things sort of overlap. But to contribute knowledge in almost any area requires some type of group collaboration, with multiple people, and different kinds of artificial intelligences."

"Now your group, four of you together, are you together for long?"

"We've been stabilized in this configuration for five years. And we'll see what happens as we go along."

"But you can think your mind there now. What happens to the four of you eventually?"

"I can't precisely predict the future, but projections indicate that we stay together for another two and half years. After that we 'transition'. One of us will join another group. The remaining three will continue on and be joined by another."

I wanted to find out if I was part of the group. Almost as immediately as the question formed in my mind, I received an answer inside me saying, 'no'. Tim and I, as close as we naturally feel with one another, are not from the same soul group.

But I wanted a confirmation from Ramrut, "I need you to think about an answer to the following question: The soul that is known as Kemila, does she have a presence there on the Ring?"

"I don't think I can answer that question. That is from a completely different plane, a different existence than where I am."

"So how does life end?" I was not sure if I should call it "end of life", or death, as I was not even sure if that label would be appropriate for the Ring life.

"I will become part of a group when nothing is left for me as an individual."

"So, you just ... merge, and become part of the group?"

"Yes."

"How do you do that?" *Isn't all death a sort of merging, transitioning from one consciousness to another?*

"I go and lie down. There is a force supporting me. And I will open myself to the group I have chosen, and instantly leave this body behind."

That's my dream death! "Tell me more about the group you've chosen. Why did you choose that group?"

"It's difficult to explain, but different groups have different values and interests. We understand this almost from a kind of emotional perspective, rather than an analytical one. Like, how do you fall in love?"

"Maybe through natural bonding?"

"Yes. When you can open yourself up in small ways for small periods of time, you can gain a sense of how others resonate with your frequency."

"So, the group you chose resonates with you."

"Yes, it feels good."

"If I were to come to visit your group, how would you describe the characteristics of it? How would you introduce your group to me?"

"It feels like they have a curious heart."

"Now this group with a curious heart, that you chose to go back to merge with, how many of such groups are there?"

"It's a different realm. There are many, but this group mind itself interacts with other group minds, and they can join with others, or split ... It's entirely different realms ..."

I gave Ramrut a further suggestion, "You will know more after you merge back to the group ..."

But I was interrupted, "I will. Not he." Right. I thought to myself, of course, Ramrut had already merged, or transitioned.

"Is it the group mind speaking with me now?" I wondered if Tim's, or Ramrut's, terminology "group minds" was what we'd call "oversouls". A divinely fundamental or elemental unity that transcends both duality and multiplicity.

"Yes."

"What was the lesson learned through the experience as Ramrut?"

"People and relations are magical. So much more than just the sum of the parts. Now we are complete. Somehow. Like becoming a butterfly."

With that, the session came to a close. Whomever it was in front of me, a euphoric feeling came over that entity. And there appeared to be no desire to answer any of my further questions. Each response was the same as the last:

"Just *be*."

17

New York, New York

By the end of summer 2012, Tim and I had completed three past life regressions on the life of Carol Benjamin. I did not think there would be anything major left that we could dig out of that lifetime. It was an interesting life and Carol was certainly a character Tim and I both enjoyed reliving and learning about. In our random conversations we would frequently and fondly joke about her.

One day near summer's end, Tim and I had an argument. It was one of those easily forgettable couples' arguments, where you wonder what it had been all about. Afterwards, I went off to work in my office at home. When I finally came out, I found a little note on the dining table:

> Honey,
>
> I've gone out to watch the 2nd half of the championship football game. I'll eat in the bar.
>
> I'm sorry we fought. As you say though, it adds spice. But I love you. I'll always love you. Remember that, through all conceptions of time.
>
> Tim/Carol

Tim knew that in signing it that way it would put a smile on my face and ease the tension from our spat. But he could not have known what signing in that manner would foretell.

> Honey,
>
> I've gone out to watch the 2nd half of the championship football game. I'll eat in the bar.
>
> I'm sorry we fought. As you say though, it adds spice. But I love you. I'll always love you. Remember that Trrugh all conceptions of time.
>
> Tim/Carol.

A month after Tim/Carol's make-up letter, a friend who had moved to New York City for work invited us to join him and his family on a trip to see the Fall foliage in New England. Tim and I both felt it would be much more interesting to visit New York City, than to see the changing Autumn colours of the Massachusetts trees. We suggested to our friend that we simply visit him for a week in Manhattan instead, to which he readily agreed.

For the previous two years, I had been exchanging hypnotherapy sessions with my colleague Korë. We had both enjoyed doing sessions for each other, we both benefited from them enormously. As it turned out, a week before my trip to New York City, I was again working with Korë. Towards the end of the session, Korë's spirit guide came forth uttering words of wisdom involving different aspects of her life. I had been sensing that something was going to come up on my trip, but I did not know quite what it was. So, on a hunch, I tossed out a question of my own to Korë's guide, "I am going to New York next week. Is there anything you can share with me about it?"

After a quick scan, Korë's facial expression became amused, and her guide responded, "Oh, New York. Very interesting … Very, very bright! And very, very dark! You will have a most interesting time there."

Naturally, I had thought Korë's guide was referring to the brightness of the city's skyline, and the darkness of its criminal underbelly. Or, at least something similar. It never occurred to me that Korë's spirit guide was being completely literal!

It was to be my first trip to New York—at least in this lifetime. And I easily adapted my work schedule for this somewhat impromptu trip. But as our departure drew nearer, I could not help but begin to recall the names of places that had come up during our sessions exploring Carol's lifetime.

Tim and I embarked on that New York trip full of anticipation. It would be both a holiday visiting good friends, and a chance to discover, in this life, some of the places from Tim's past life as Carol. I was curious whether he would have any memories triggered by the places we planned to visit.

Our dear friends lived halfway up a twenty-story, red brick, high-rise that was part of a large residential development in Stuyvesant Town-Peter Cooper Village. Stuyvesant Town turned out to be a pleasant area near the East River that was full of leafy green trees and pedestrian walkways.

We arrived in town late on a Friday evening. Almost instantly, my friends asked us a little concerned: "Have you seen the weather forecast?" We told them not to worry, we knew the forecast for much of the week would be rain, but that was fine. Coming from Vancouver we were long since accustomed to wet weather. Besides which, we were visiting a metropolis that had much to offer regardless of the weather. Before the rain came, Tim and I intended to focus our activities out-of-doors, and then spend those rainy days in museums and galleries, visiting little bars and cafes, and generally enjoying the typical Big Apple experience. But, little did we know how far from the "typical" our experience would prove to be.

The weather it turned out, was not just any rainy weather. It was blustering and deadly tropical storm weather. Hurricane Sandy was going to turn our little vacation into an adventure in more ways than one.

We had arrived two days before the storm hit and prior to the city being shut down. Exploring for Carol's old haunts quickly took a backseat to simply being able to see what we could see. The first day we spent a lovely autumn morning in Central Park with our friends. After we parted ways, Tim and I found ourselves walking blissfully along the streets of Manhattan. We wandered into Grand Central Terminal. Surprisingly, it was grander and more bustling than even the movies depict. Inside the immense hall, the strangest thing happened to Tim. He became overwhelmed as he gazed about dazedly. Slowly he turned to me, "I'm not sure what it is. I'm feeling something here, like déjà-vu. Could you leave me alone for a moment?"

Tim had never asked me to "leave him alone". That was the very first time, and the only time. I walked away and from a respectful distance, I kept a watchful eye on my partner the whole time. I realized a sudden and quite powerful recognition of sorts must have flooded his mind, body, and senses. I was positive it had something to do with Carol's life, but I wanted to let him sort it out for himself, if he could. It also dawned on me that up until that moment, Tim still did not fully believe in the "past life stuff".

I waited patiently until I saw him obviously looking around for me, trying to seek out my familiar face in the crowd.

Tim had not managed to sort anything out, but he had allowed the unsettling feelings to subside.

The following morning, we made the long subway ride up to Harlem to take in a traditional Gospel choir in one of the Baptist churches there.

Turning on our phone after the service, there was an urgent message from our friends warning us that the subways would shut down at four that afternoon. Tim and I made it back to their neighbourhood just in the nick of time. The subways uncharacteristically shut down, and the storm winds began to blow.

❦ ❦ ❦ ❦

Hurricane Sandy was determined to make the history books with winds gusting at upwards of 80 km/hour. It was the strongest and most destructive tropical storm in America since Hurricane Katrina. The city and its surrounding areas were left utterly devastated. Being without power, half of Manhattan was stranded in darkness. Subways and roads were inundated by flooding from the storm surge along the coastline. The airports were closed; all scheduled flights having been grounded. Our friends, as it turned out, lived in the southern half of the island, the half *without* power.

No power meant a sudden return to the Dark Ages: no phone service, no Internet, and as we soon discovered, no water, as the high-rises relied on electrical pumps. Our friend's post-World War II building lacked a back-up generator. Thankfully, the pumps were magically powered for several hours each day, during which time we would fill all our friend's available containers with water. Coming or going from their apartment entailed a long hike up, or down, a pitch-dark stairwell lit only a few feet in front of us by the light of our phones.

Nobody knew when things would get back to normal. Even in the half of Manhattan with power, many places were closed due to transportation issues. Our sightseeing plans had come to an abrupt halt, our flights home cancelled.

I had prescheduled some workshops I was teaching and was desperate to rebook myself onto *any* flight back to Vancouver as soon as I could, to honour my commitments. I asked Tim to remain behind and catch our original return flight that was delayed. The flight I had arranged was not at all a convenient route. Tim said plainly, "There's nothing for me here in New York City without you."

Given what unfolded during the superstorm and its aftermath, Tim's simple statement brought both tears to my weary eyes and warmed my saddened heart.

It was 4am. And we had carefully picked our way downstairs from the tenth floor, toting our luggage with us, the glow of our phones' flashlights our only guide. An airport shuttle had been booked and we had been told to wait out front of the building for it. Everything seemed so surreal. This was Manhattan, the City of Lights. Yet the sole source of light in that pitch-dark world was the eerie luminescence of the full moon overhead. The last few days had been challenging, to say the least, and we were overcome from the unexpected harshness of events. We worried whether the shuttle would be able to find its way to us in the darkness and chaos. We fretted whether our flight out of Newark International Airport would make it out, taking us back to safety, taking us home.

It was a strange and conflicted farewell.

New York, we so love you. Yet we are so desperately trying to get away from you.

18

Shelter from the Storm

When life throws a hurricane at you what do you do? For us, inspired both by the city and Tim's Grand Central Station flashback, we opted for a past life regression. It was the evening after we had returned from Harlem. Tim chose to lie comfortably on the bed in our friends' modestly furnished guest room, while I sat cross-legged beside him on the bed, close to his head. In the background, we could hear the cheerful sounds of our friends' small family talking and playing together in the living room. And the ever-busy New York traffic humming in accompaniment to the shifting pitch of sirens, that created a wailing arpeggio in the night.

Lying down in bed easily created a relaxing feeling for Tim. So, I decided to use a quick induction into that past life with which we had become so familiar. It took roughly three minutes. I had Tim imagine being in a large water park. I told him that he was standing on top of a waterslide where there was a large faucet. By turning the handle of the faucet, he could control which past life he would emerge into—and of course, Tim wished to return to the lifetime that had *every*thing to do with the very city that we were in, the lifetime that we had visited three times before, the life of Carol Benjamin.

As Tim turned the handle in his imagination, I counted backwards from 10 to 1. He sat down in the waterslide chute and slid backward in time, backward into the lifetime that his subconscious mind had already chosen.

It made me laugh that this fun-filled induction had guided Tim directly to a moment in Carol's childhood. Carol was merely seven years old and riding her bike alongside her friends. The children were at Carol's Long Island summer home.

I had decided for myself that this session was to focus primarily on the facts alone. If we could identify verifiable facts, then Tim would have to accept that at least some of what we discovered in our life regressions and progressions were real, and not simply his active imagination. He had not seemed completely satisfied with his discovery of Chestnut Street. Yes, such a street had existed at the time, but looking at where it was on the map, Tim was not sure that would have been a residential neighbourhood.

I directed 7-year-old Carol, "Go to the front door of the house. Carol, can you read numbers?"

"Of course, I can. I could read numbers before any of my friends." Her child's voice filled with pride.

"Good for you! Now Carol, go to the front door, if there is a number there, or if there is a number on the fence, read it now."

Just as I finished posing my question to Carol, our friend walked past the guest bedroom door, speaking loudly to his wife as he went.

"What was that?" Carol asked.

I had to desensitize Tim. "Nothing. Just come back to the house Carol, and focus on the sound of my voice, anything else you may hear is not important. What is there, at the house?" I had meant the number on the door, or fence that the young Carol was supposed to find. But, true to the casual and carefree nature of children, she quickly found her friends, her bicycle, and off she went.

I discovered that Carol at seven could be as petulant and stubborn as an older Carol sipping cocktails in Cuba. She was far more interested in riding her bike with her friends than in looking for the address of her home. When I finally did get her to return home, Carol seemed to get bored, and Tim tired. However, I did learn that they had a maid named Jenny, and that the house was located somewhere in the Hamptons out on Long Island.

The resistance or inability to answering simple factual questions can often happen in past life regressions. People will come in with a conscious agenda and a curiosity about the facts. But for the unconscious mind, names, addresses, years, and other facts are less relevant. The unconscious mind remembers things which have emotional imprints—the stronger the emotional experience, the easier and more vivid the memories. Even in our current lives, chances are we all have some vivid childhood memories. There will almost certainly be emotions attached to those memories. And yet, at the same time, we can struggle to remember simple things like old phone numbers, addresses, and even the names of faces we recognize in old faded photographs.

Exceptions, however, can occur when there are very intense negative emotions, such as fear and trauma. In those cases, some of the memories and their details may be blocked despite the presence of intense emotions. Likewise, some names may clearly stand out in the deep recesses of the subconscious mind as a marker or trigger.

Abandoning the address of the summer house, I next moved Carol to an older age, where she immediately found herself in a bar. She was 21. That's our Carol! I sighed to myself.

She was with three other friends, and Denise was one of them. "Is this a bar you regularly go to Carol?"

"Not often. I prefer Friday's."

"Where is Friday's?"

"It's in the Theater District, not that far from Times Square."

"Which street?"

"I don't know exactly. I just know where to go."

That is just like Tim. He had already been living in the same place for over ten years when I moved in, yet he didn't even know where many of his neighbourhood streets were actually located. He could drive to destinations across the city without knowing their actual address, nor the names of many of the roads that he traveled. Many of us navigate like that, solely by landmarks and a sense of direction.

I decided to change the topic again, to one that I knew would perk Carol up.

"Alright Carol. What I am going to do is count from 5 to 1. We are going to move now to a very interesting time in your life." I had observed that the topic of Rick always lit up Carol/Tim's face, and this might be a perfect way to get Carol engaged again. "It's okay to have some memories about that part of your life because it is an enticing period in your life. So, we are going to go to the place and time when you first met a man who we call Rick. Alright, 5 … 4 … 3 …"

A big smile climbed across Tim's face. While I was slowly counting, Tim's left hand and arm started to move, as if his left hand had a mind of its own, stretching the fingers as a sort of an antenna. Slowly, the fingers reached in the direction of my voice, as if searching for something. I sat there, watching his hand and fingers moving ever so slowly, stunned. Knowing something was about to take place, my body froze.

I continued to count to number 1, and said, "You are there now. Where is it?"

Tim's hand continued to move, sensing, seeking, reaching. On another level of his awareness, Tim as Carol was still carrying on a conversation with me, she answered, "In a village bar. It's close to where I live."

I was mystified. I could not move.

"Is his hand looking for mine?" I asked myself inwardly.

"Yes." I heard my inward answer.

I was transfixed, I couldn't do anything else but watch Tim's unconscious movement. Finally, Tim's fingers reached mine, grabbing hold of them. The smile on his face broadened. In that instant, a lightbulb went off in my mind. I knew, exactly, *finally*, how our destinies bridged together in that Manhattan lifetime.

"In a village bar. When is it?" I asked Carol, my mouth nearly dry.

"Evening time."

I recalled from an earlier session, that Carol had told me she and Rick had met in a little diner. Carol confirmed now that she was only there for a drink, and Rick had happened to drop in on his own as well. He offered to buy Carol a drink. That was the dawning of their story. Carol was 23 at the time.

"Carol, what attracts you to Rick?" This question started to take on a deeper meaning more than ever now.

"I don't know. He's kind of … He's carefree but he's so intense. He is focused, and he laughs. And he's good-looking. And that smile …" Tim had a dreamy look on his face.

Carefree. Intense. Focused. Laughing. Good-looking. How would I live up to that description now, I wondered?

"And what attracted him to you?"

Briefly, Carol was silent and then answered innocently, "How would I know that?"

I laughed. This sure sounded very Tim.

I reminded myself that the whole session was not to be story oriented, but facts oriented. Since we were already in New York City, I wanted to extract as much data as possible, so I could see if I could verify them later. Quickly, I shifted Carol again.

"Just go to the last time you and Rick met each other. Where is it and when is it?"

I knew Rick was absent in Carol's life soon after Carol had become a mother. I wanted to know how and when they parted, though.

Little was I to know this line of questioning would bear forth layers of dense emotions, emotions which would remain for the rest of our New York stay.

After a long pause, Carol found the information that was buried deep in her subconscious memory, "We're in a little midtown coffee shop."

"How old are you now Carol?"

"31." That would make the year 1933, and Rick, the centurial baby, would be 33 years old.

"The coffee shop is the last time you meet. Whose idea was it to meet there?"

"Mine." Carol released a big sigh.

"It was your idea to meet there. Was it because you wanted to break up with him?"

"No. We haven't seen much of each other lately."

"You mean for months or years?"

"Not since The Crash."

The Crash! My heart sank, all the way to the bottom. Yes, of course I remembered the stock market crash, those dark and gloomy days. Flashbacks haunted my childhood memories.

Carol continued, "It wiped him out."

Every word pinched my heart.

"So, Rick is not in very good shape right now?"

"He is very … down." Carol's voice sounded forlorn. "I don't know what I can do! I want to help. I've already given him some money. But he didn't even want to accept it. I don't know what else I can do. He told me just to go away and leave him alone!"

"He is a proud man, isn't he?" I knew it, didn't I?

"Yes." And I knew well enough that if Rick were asking her to leave him alone, there really wasn't anything that Carol could do about it.

"Does he have any other plans?"

"I think he wants to end it all, to kill himself."

Foreseeably, Rick would think suicide was the only easy way out. And in that instant, I *knew* that was how Rick died.

I had known the me-Rick soul had had other suicidal lifetimes. Characteristically, always choosing an early exit when despair consumed them. It was our way of pushing the reset button, as if life were a video game.

In my early teens, I remembered telling my friends that I would likely end up killing myself. I had shared this in a very calm, matter-of-fact way, using much the same tone that my peers would use when relaying how they would become a doctor, teacher, or lawyer when they grew up. It had startled my friends, which in turn had surprised me. What was the big deal with this life, anyway? I did not have a reason to kill myself yet, but also could not find anything wrong with that idea, either.

"That's why you never saw Rick again after your coffee shop meeting?" I inquired.

"That's why. Yes."

"After that day, did you try to reach out to him, to contact him again?"

Again, there was another long pause. Poor Carol, she was in obvious pain!

I decided to come at it differently, "Did you ever find any information about him after that?" Our friends out in the living room burst out laughing. The family was probably enjoying a board game together. But, in that intense moment I had an unforgiving urge to go out there and kill them, regardless of us being guests in their home.

"Maybe soon after?" I ventured, adding onto my previous question.

Carol sighed, deeply. "No. I didn't see or hear from him ever again. And I didn't learn anything about him for a long time after that. It was not until several years later that I heard he went to California. He'd killed himself there."

"When did he go there? What did he do in California?"

"He went there in 1933. I don't know what he did there, though." That was the same year that Rick and Carol met for the last time. The year he had asked her to leave him alone. I thought sadly that he would not have had much time to start a new life there if he took his own life later that same year.

"Carol, how did Rick kill himself?"

Tim looked even more distraught than before. His eyes were squeezed shut, tears forming in the corners. Time passed and yet stood still.

"He hung himself."

I searched frantically for oxygen in my body, and in my mind. But in that second, I was not sure if my soul wanted to stay or leave.

Desperately needing any verbal confirmation from Carol/Tim, I asked, "Now if Rick's personality reminds you of anyone in this life of Tim, who would that be?"

After a brief pause, an eternity, he said, "*You.*"

❦   ❦   ❦   ❦

Deep down I had been feeling it, and now, here was Tim saying it aloud. I was Rick. I *was* Rick. Questions bounced around my head, ricocheting off one another as I tried to get them out. I asked whether Carol and Rick had done other trips together like they had to Havana. They hadn't. Being a married woman meant it was not easy for Carol to travel often, or easily with a man who was not her husband.

I asked about jazz music and the clubs they used to haunt. Did Tim's fondness for jazz extend to Carol's life, when jazz first sashayed into the clubs of the nineteen twenties and thirties? It had. Rick and Carol had first begun frequenting a small club called the Backdoor, and later the legendary Cotton Club, made famous by Louis Armstrong, Duke Ellington, and the like. I marvelled at what it must have been like to see and hear these artists live and in colour. But quickly appreciated that I probably had, only in a different lifetime.

My questions were boundless. I wanted to know where Carol had lived and where Mark had worked. As it turned out, Mark had once considered moving his office to the Empire State Building before deciding to move downtown.

Did the Empire State Building already exist in Carol's life? I made a note to research it later.

"That is the tallest building in the world!" Carol continued her retrospection, excitedly. "It was in all the newspapers when it opened. So tall!"

"Have you been there Carol?"

"Oh yeah!"

"Did you go all the way to the top?"

"Yes, up to the observation deck."

I jumped to the subject of her children next, hoping Tim and I would be able to trace some of Carol's descendants in our post-regression fact finding. But my questions lacked any coherence, they bounced around like an uncontrollable yo-yo ball. Eager and inexperienced as I was, I was treating Tim/Carol like an automated information center. Carol began to frown. Realizing that my rapid-fire interviewing approach had been a mistake, I decided to give Carol a break, but ...

"Is there anything else you can tell me about Anne?"

After a little reticent pause, "I don't know if I should."

"That's alright, Carol. You can tell me."

"I have always thought that Rick is her father."

What?!

I could not believe my ears. "Rick is Anne's biological father?"

"I don't know for sure, but I think so, yes. She has his spark and she reminds me of him in so many ways. The timing certainly works."

"You knew or suspected that ever since she was born?"

Carol nodded her head.

"Did Rick ever know about it? Did he ever meet Anne?"

"No, I never said anything to him. Maybe I should have. Maybe if he'd known …" Dispirited, Carol's voice trailed off.

"So, you kept the secret. Is that the reason why you have always felt closer to Anne? Or is it just because Anne is Anne?" I remembered from our previous sessions, how Carol had shown a tendency in singling out Anne whenever left or encouraged to describe her children.

"I love both my children. But yes, Anne holds a special place in my heart. She reminds me of a past that is gone, but she also lets me glimpse an alternate future. Her independence, striving to follow her own path. I was a little crazy when I was young. I was rebellious, so is Anne."

I didn't know where Carol was going with this line of thought, but she continued, "What happened with Rick … I was … It was really hard on me for a while. I thought that I knew who I was and then suddenly, I didn't. Or at least I did not like the person I realized I had become. I'd taken so much for granted. Both Rick and Mark. They both deserved better. Gradually, as the pain subsided, I became determined to be a better person. And I did."

"Anne's rebelliousness reminds you of your younger days?" It was ironic in a way since those whom children often rebel against are their parents, yet here was Carol admiring that.

"Yes. But she also showed me a different path of rebellion."

"If it were not for your traffic accident, you would conceivably have seen her finish growing up, seen what she would have made of her life."

Carol nodded. Tears were back in the corners of her eyes.

With that intriguing news, I needed to know more. I no longer cared now. Forget about the "last" question. Consequently, a whole flood of new questions emerged. Slowly and steadily I teased the story from Carol.

Rick had never gotten to know his daughter. He had never been aware of her existence in relation to him. Due to the timing of Carol's pregnancy, he may have suspected, but Carol, fearing her own security, had outright denied the fact the one-time Rick had enquired.

With the birth of Anne, however, Carol was completely torn. She found herself in a perilous tug-o-war with motherhood and her social life, her husband and her lover, with fear and hope itself. At first, she had coped well, balancing two lives and new responsibilities with relative ease. Being able to afford a nanny for a while, simplified navigating her marriage, motherly duties, and maintaining her affair with Rick. Perhaps the nanny suspected something, they usually do. But she never said anything, and Carol never asked.

Then the market crash of 1929 changed everything. The nanny could no longer be kept on, and Carol could no longer see Rick as much as before. Yet that was the time Rick most needed someone, or so Carol thought. With no job and little money, Rick became alone and almost destitute. It was increasingly difficult to sustain contact. They drifted apart until that last heartbreaking meeting in a midtown coffee shop.

It would take another lifetime, *this* lifetime, to have the truth of Anne revealed to me. I swiftly did the math again in my head. Anne could be alive in the year 2012. If so, she would be around 90 years old.

It was time to count Tim back to our current reality, back to the same New York City we were in, back to our friend's apartment that was sheltering us from the tempest at our door. Matching our own black and heavy emotions, New York, the city that never sleeps, was also about to be plunged thoroughly and frightfully into darkness.

19

The Fear of Living

Wandering down the Manhattan streets with Tim, I felt a strange interplay of emotions; Rick's despair was palpable, but so was my love, and yes, fear of New York. The energy of the city's skyscrapers, busy streets, fast-moving crowds, and neon lights, all called upon my soul's memory. I was both euphorically elated and hopelessly desperate; left entirely drained, yet completely satisfied.

It was two days after the past life regression, and we were queued in line for the observatory deck to the Empire State Building. Hurricane Sandy had crippled the city. Half of Manhattan was still without electricity. But we planned to tour and sightsee what we could at places that had electricity and were open to the public.

Like a Russian ballet, the Empire State Building tour was perfectly choreographed. Where to wait, where to stand, what to do, what comes next; the staff must have performed this flawless ritual a thousand times over. It felt like being treated like a number, but the rhythm and the pace of it made it seem oddly comfortable. I imagined how Carol must have gone through the very same building 70 years earlier—what she had seen, how she had felt. In this life, Tim and I were no longer Carol and Rick. Now we had different roles and genders, different names, possessed different shapes and sizes, and cultures. But the building, the building remained resolutely the same.

Getting off on the 80th floor, we changed elevators in order to reach our final destination of the 86th floor and the Observatory Deck. Walking idly around this crossover floor, I browsed the surrounding gift shops and exhibits. Displayed in the hall on square pillars were black and white photographs of old New York cityscapes. Mindlessly scanning the images, I suddenly stopped. Signaling to Tim to come over and join me, I pointed at one particular pillar.

Tim's gaze followed my finger. As if an electrical current had just shocked him, he jerked and shook his head, as if fighting against a trance. Blinking furiously, he tried to remain conscious and focused.

On the pillar stood a photo of a café with a neon sign. The sign read, *Friday's.*

I knew Tim had already forgotten many of the facts Carol had told me in hypnosis, likely including Friday's. While he remembers most of Carol's stories, he does not necessarily retain all the details of those memories. Yet looking at that simple black and white photograph in an Empire State Building exhibit, Tim seemed to be transported to a different time. Momentarily lifted out of time … past-life déjà-vu.

Finally, we made our way up to the Observatory Deck. It was nothing short of incredible! Looking down from the Observatory Deck, a jagged east-west line was centered almost perfectly on the Empire State Building itself. Places to the north, like Times Square, had electricity and were as vibrant and lively as can ever be. But towards the south, everything was precariously dark. Standing there overlooking the city in wonder, New York had become a city of two tales, in more sense than one.

Korë's spirit guide's voice reappeared in my ears, *"Oh, New York ... Very, very bright! And very, very dark! You will have a most interesting time there."*

Very interesting indeed!

Tim is our household photojournalist, always busy snapping a multitude of photos whenever we travel. But in that moment on top of the Empire State Building, facing the stark contrast of pitch darkness and brilliant light laid out before us, Tim didn't want to take any photos.

So, we just stood still, hand in hand, shoulder to shoulder, marvelling at how special the moment was, where the brightest city had become the darkest void.

And remembering Carol and Rick, we realized how overdue this moment had been.

❖   ❖   ❖   ❖

When we finally did return home to Vancouver, I immediately stopped volunteering at the palliative care program. I had come to understand that death and dying had never been a fear I needed to overcome. The fear had been about living, and what it was to truly *live* a life. Admitting that to myself eased both some tension and the fear itself.

So many times, when doing the most ordinary things in life, completely without warning, I would become anxious and panicky. Now it clicked. I had a fear of living!

It made more sense to face my own fear than to continue doing what was easier, dancing with death. I decided I would use those same Sunday afternoons to walk in the park by our home, feel the trees, and feel the *aliveness* in and of Nature.

Hey John, now I have found there is something better to do than watching people die on Sunday afternoons.

Even though we may plan and think in our very human analytical, rational, and problem-solving way, everything has its own pattern, rhythm, and timing. Many times, I have asked myself why Tim and I came together at all, and why at that precise moment. There were times when I used to dream about being with a partner who traveled and attended the same spiritual workshops and events with me, with whom I could discuss the same things that excited us both.

But exactly at the moment I had first met Tim, my life had been undergoing a massive transformational shift. I started drifting away from many of the things I used to care about, causing my interests to become narrower and more focused. By the same token, I felt if we had met earlier, I could have made myself a better partner for him. I knew I was becoming more authentically Kemila, a person truer to herself, but I simply could not fathom the timing of it all. It felt unfair that Tim had to suffer from my lack of interests in the many things that interested him, like art and science and politics.

"You are only interested in the topic of hypnosis, nothing else." Tim would complain, in a stifled tone.

Sorry baby. But I am truly not interested in anything else. Maybe it is genetic. Maybe I have the hypnosis gene. I just can't help myself.

That simply was not true, though. I love travelling, still. On that Canada Day when we first met, it was that subject that had glued Tim and I to the blanket when everyone else was dancing in David Lam Park. And in the years to come, life and circumstances would see us travelling a great deal more together. Perhaps we are both genetically predisposed to travel?

In his life as Carol, she had dreamt that she and Rick would travel to Paris and was disappointed when he was too busy to take her. One night in the spring of 2015, as Tim lay in our hotel bed in Paris, I let him listen to a 3-minute clip recorded from the same regression where Carol had been longing for Paris.

It is never too late to realize a dream, even if it means revisiting it in another lifetime.

20

Richard Miller

"Daytime. Inside. With 5 other people". It was three weeks after our surreal visit to New York, and Tim had just started our fifth regression into the life of Carol Benjamin. He had easily agreed to do this session with me, having been told its focus would be on the life of Rick.

Rick's loneliness, angst, passion, regret, and most importantly, his (and my) determination for a change of perception on the idea of loss, lingered with me still.

In the weeks prior to the session, I had gone into a hypnotic state twice by using my own *Past Life Regression* CD, with the intention of accessing Rick's life on my own. An image of a tall, lean man with brown hair, appearing confident and carefree, who liked wearing light coloured leather loafers, had appeared to me. Nevertheless, a deep sadness seemed to permeate his soul.

I had felt a strong urge to reach out to this vision of Rick. But during those few self-hypnosis sessions, something stood between us. Maybe it was his pride, or maybe it was mine; was there even a difference between the two?

Tim lay on the couch, his favourite position, and I stood by his side. Holding his hand up, I had him study my face. My facial features, the contours of my jaw, and the outlines of my mouth and nose. Lastly, I had him gaze into my eyes. Counting slowly backward from twenty, I gave Tim the suggestion that his eyelids were becoming heavier and heavier, but he could still see my eyes, and could still look deeply into them. As if "the eyes you see extend into another dimension, a tunnel taking you all the way to a time where you know these same eyes." Isn't it often said that our eyes are the windows to the soul? When I reached the number zero, I gently pulled his hand, and commanded, "Deep sleep!"

On cue, Tim's eyes shut, and I dropped his hand to the couch by his side. "Deeper now ... and deeper ... all the way down ... Travelling through that tunnel, into that same lifetime where you met and knew those pair of eyes ..."

"Is it daytime or nighttime, are you inside or outside, alone or with someone?"

"Daytime. Inside. With 5 other people," came Carol's response.

She was in her mid 40's and sitting in a meeting with five others. Carol only seemed to know one of them, her husband's friend Paul. It was an organizing meeting for a young artist's gallery showing. While Carol was not familiar with this artist, she did regularly volunteer her time in coordinating, promoting, and liaising with different groups to raise greater awareness of gifted young artists. And the work proved to be a fitting way for Carol to network and meet new people.

I recalled that Carol herself painted, so I asked her, "Have you ever displayed your own artwork in any gallery?"

"No, my work isn't worth showing."

"But you did hang up some of your artwork at home, didn't you?"

"Yes."

"But you don't think they are good enough to be exhibited in public?"

"What I do is not the same as the kind of artists that I'm passionate about. They are at the frontier of pushing art forward. I paint simple landscapes."

In a way, Tim is similar. He can be obsessive about his photography and in upgrading his camera gear. Often, when we are out walking or exploring, he will carry his camera with him, his thoughts easily flowing towards the quality of the light and how to capture the best shots. Later, at home, he will spend endless moments going through his photographs one by one, tweaking them in his image editing program until he is satisfied with the outcome.

Sometimes, upon seeing his camera, people would ask if he is a photographer. He would quickly respond that he was not. And I would just as quickly add, "Yes, he is."

Tim does not share his pictures much, generally keeping them to himself. I would get so frustrated at his unwillingness towards sharing his craft with a wider audience. Perhaps, it is because the idea of hobbies and pastimes have a slightly different practice and connotation for me, but I could not understand how people could put so much time and energy into doing something without sharing with a bigger audience. He could justify that by saying he did it just for the simple pleasure of doing them. I saw it as fear of being judged. Since you are already doing something, you might as well profit from it and turn it into a business, or at least share it freely. But neither Tim nor Carol felt the same way.

Maybe Carol was correct in thinking that her art was not good enough. Or, maybe this has been the soul's challenge in multiple lifetimes: To put their work out there.

I continued to ask Carol, "Let's go to the show now … How does the show turn out?"

"Reasonably well."

"Have you met any interesting people there?"

"Hmmm … Not really."

Forty-six-year-old Carol had become a completely different person from the early twenties' version. Now she was a model woman of her time: a good mother, good wife, and upstanding member in her social circles. Regardless, inside it seemed, something of the Carol essence had died. Boredom seeped through the voice lying on the couch.

"Carol, are there other things that you do besides promoting artists?"

"Yes, I do other things. I'm well connected, so I bring people together for different projects." With that, Carol realized something, and she chuckled.

"What is it?" I asked.

"All those years of ... socializing ... kind of came together in this regard."

I laughed as well. "How interesting! What you did before has ..."

"... found some value!" Carol finished my sentence with more laughter.

I wanted to turn our focus on Rick, though. So I guided Carol back to "one of those afternoons in September 1925". That was, according to what I knew, when she was frequently spending time with Rick. But Carol quickly corrected me, "Mostly in the evenings."

"Okay. Evenings. Where do you normally see Rick?"

"His place, or clubs."

"How often do the two of you get together?"

"About three times a week."

Rick, or Richard Miller, was born May 17, 1900, and grew up extremely poor. His grandparents had emigrated from Eastern Europe to America in the 1800s. But upon their arrival in a new land, his grandparents discovered that the immigration officers in New York could not pronounce their Eastern European surname. Or perhaps, in an effort to assimilate and blend in, his grandparents had changed their name to the more Anglicized "Miller".

Rick was an only child who never experienced having a happy and healthy relationship with his parents. They were very tough on him, having unreasonably high expectations and beating him often. Rick hated his parents with a passion, he had no intention of being like them. Rather, he had a burning desire to be better, to be far wealthier than who he came from. With that fervid motivation smoldering at his core, the finance industry seemed a natural choice for him.

"Carol, tell me more about Rick. Does he enjoy working on Wall Street?"

"Very much! He makes good money. And he likes the excitement of it."

"Throughout the years, what stopped you from leaving your husband and getting together with Rick?"

"That is … really complicated. I guess there are two of me inside … Part of me needs freedom to have fun and be carefree. But, another part of me needs the peace of having security and stability."

"Rick doesn't provide security and stability? At least not the way a lawyer does, is that it?"

"Rick himself doesn't mind the situation. He doesn't want to settle down."

I supposed that Rick would likely not have married Carol even if she had divorced Mark.

"Why did you marry Mark, since you don't love him much?"

"It was the easiest way to get out of my parents place. I hated living there. It was too restrictive. I was 20 years old. Anyways, they expected me to marry Mark."

"So, after you married Mark, the fun started. Mark was hardworking and easy going. You started going out drinking, dancing, and partying. Wait a minute …" I suddenly thought of something. It was the nineteen twenties. "Carol, isn't alcohol banned?"

Carol gave me a good chuckle. "The days of prohibition were when I drank the most."

"Isn't it illegal?"

"The more it's prohibited, the more fun we had!"

I could see a lot of Carol in Tim. 'Fun' is a word that speaks to Tim all the time.

On the carefree level, Carol and Rick connected. Growing up with uptight and overbearing parents, Carol could not completely disregard what was expected of her gender and social class. So being a good wife and a good mother were equally important to her, even though like many a new mother, she struggled with caring for her children at the beginning.

For Rick, it was not just the loss of his money that was so devastating. Growing up in poverty, he knew what living on the edge was all about. No, it was the loss of hope. On some level he likely knew he could survive and recoup his financial position. The Crash, however, mentally threw him off balance, utterly and completely. As a proud man, it stole his spirit and he never recovered. There really wasn't much left for him to hold on to.

I know, in this life, I can easily dramatize financial and physical loss. It is a dark hole that I try hard not to fall into. In a strange way, I feel extremely grateful to Rick. As if, knowing of his short 33-years of life, I have someone to guide me, signaling a direction *not* to go in. It has granted me a peaceful sense of support in living this life now.

Yet I often wonder, what are the causes and effects of me doing hypnotherapy work in this lifetime? I know I have had other lifetimes as a spiritual teacher, an advisor, and other types of mystics. I pondered how Rick's life fit into my soul's grand design. Rick who had worked on one of the most crowded American streets, in one of the most crowded cities, in one of the most thriving countries, failed miserably. What does it add to the bigger picture? And what does it have for me as Kemila to learn?

And if Rick's life had not been ended so young, would he be doing something similar to what I was doing now? After all, Carol matured dramatically in the latter part of her life. And I did not start doing what I am now doing until I turned forty.

I can accept that my work is the continuation of work I have done in previous lifetimes. My travels are the absolute definition of my soul's expression, throughout any lifetime. But on a personal level, and in this life, I was needful of healing in one key aspect of my being. When Tim first met me, I was working at a private investment company. Optimistically, I had invested much of my savings into my company's products and its partner companies. My optimism was contagious. After meeting me, Tim also invested a lot of his own savings into these same products. Then when the global financial crisis of 2007-08 hit, the company, like so many others, struggled. And eventually I lost my job and all my investments with it.

In the following years, I frequently felt down and confused. I dreamt of giving up on Canada and becoming a recluse in some remote area. But I had just met Tim. I could not leave him. And I was not alone in my distress, Tim was also going through some career and financial difficulties. I was not quite sure how I could make it all work.

Despite that, hypnotherapy has been my saving grace. As I made myself available to my clients, it miraculously healed me on a mental, emotional, spiritual, and financial level. Meeting people from all walks of life, learning of their challenges, I could clearly observe how the mind turns against itself and fixates on problems. I became a Master of the Obvious—through my clear seeing and perception, combined with detective skills, and my own lifetimes of experiences, I have come to understand how a maladaptive mind works, on even a mechanical level.

Many years ago, when I was living in Guangzhou, China a friend said to me, "I feel as if you are living many lifetimes in one." During the course of my current lifetime, I have changed careers, countries, relationships, interests, and my legal name. Perhaps, I needed to hurry towards something, something new and more meaningful.

In some of my most vulnerable moments, Rick still comes to mind a lot. I know him to be incredibly soft hearted, no matter how he presented himself to the world. In those moments, it is as if he is standing right there, just on the other side of my mind's eye, looking back at me and saying, "Hey, some of those things I've done, I've done for you, so that you don't have to do them anymore. You have got to go beyond and do me proud."

Sitting here by the beautiful Richelieu River in Quebec, while writing these words, so close to New York state, tears flow down my face. *I know, Rick, as they say, rest in peace. It is my turn now to do things for you in living a rich, fulfilling, courageous life with Tim.*

21

It Doesn't End

Many of my clients have commented on the peaceful artwork of a young shepherdess which hangs near the entrance of my home office. Years before we'd met, Tim had bought this reproduction of Augustus Burke's painting *A Connemara Girl* from the National Gallery of Ireland in Dublin. Many other clients have openly appreciated the two impressionistic prints displayed on the walls of the therapy room: Emily Carr's *Red Cedar* and Lawren Harris' *Lake and Mountain*. Both of them were prominent Canadian painters from the early part of the twentieth century.

Though the functionality of the room has been changed a few times over the past twenty years, and the furniture updated and moved around, especially after the space was turned into a hypnotherapy room, these two paintings have not changed their positions on the wall. It is in those moments that I cannot help but feel that maybe, in our pre-life agreement, Tim was to come in and set the stage, and I would come in and play.

In this play, I do not know where the end is.

Neither do I want one.

When I am done writing the story, the story does not cease to continue on.

⁂ ⁂ ⁂ ⁂

When I was about 14 years old, I learned my first full English song. And till this day, I still remember the full lyrics of it.

Back then we had no personal electronic devices except a transistor radio at home. The radio stations in my hometown didn't play English songs, so there was no way for me to learn any. One day at school, my class went on a Spring outing. Walking along together, my young English teacher confessed she had just learned a new song that she liked very much. I asked her to sing it to me:

> *Oh! Carol,*
> *I'm but a fool.*
> *Darling, I love you,*
> *Though you treat me cruel.*
> *You hurt me,*
> *And you make me cry.*
> *But if you leave me,*
> *I'll surely die.*
>
> *Darling, there will never be another,*
> *Cause I love you so.*
> *Don't ever leave me,*
> *Say you'll never go.*

I will always want you for my sweetheart,
No matter what you do.
Oh! Carol,
I'm so in love with you.

I was hooked. There on that day when I was 14, walking in a beautiful field of spring flowers, my English teacher taught me word for word, how to sing Neil Sedaka's, *Oh! Carol*.

✤   ✤   ✤   ✤

When Tim and I met at the Jazz Festival, one thing that had kept us glued to that blanket was the topic of travel. And since we have been together, we continue to travel the world extensively, exploring new countries and discovering new regions every year. On a lark, in many of the places we have visited, we've done past life regressions focused on that specific area. As if our travel already had its length and width predetermined, and now we were simply adding more depth to the experiences.

On the north coast of the Maltese island of Gozo, lying comfortably on a rooftop terrace under a million dazzling stars, and lolled by the balmy Mediterranean Sea, we visited Tim's 17th-century lifetime as a soldier. The soldier had grown up in the army that protected the island against the Turkish people. Rising through the ranks, he first spent many a long hour sitting high up on a cliff scouting the calm seas for ship movements. Later he was promoted to a commanding position, and was eventually killed, not by the hand of his enemies, as one would presume, but from a plot carried out by a Machiavellian comrade.

Lying on a couch in Valencia, Spain, we were introduced to the life of David, a 14th-century Andalusian soldier, who carried a big colourful flag on his horse marching to the battlefield.

On the east coast of Zanzibar, Tanzania, while gently swinging in a hammock by the Indian Ocean with a full moon lighting the skies overhead, Tim fell into a hypnotic trance, but he could not find any lifetime living on that great continent of Africa. So, I asked him to scan and see if there were any past lives for Kemila in that land. And he conveyed the most interesting story to me:

"There is an Arabic female in her mid 30's. She's along the Nile River in Northern Egypt, but South of the coast and it is lush and green. Her clothing looks sophisticated, and she is surrounded by a group of somewhat awestruck devotees who are looking up at her."

"What does she do that people are in awe of her?"

"She is a mystic, or something along that line. Maybe a priestess, like an oracle."

"She lives in a temple?"

"Yes. She is well respected. While she is privileged, her people still perceive her as kind."

"Which year does she live in? A number comes to your mind now."

"5."

"Is that it? Year 5?" I was intrigued. The number five has been the most exciting number to me since I was a child. I remember being ecstatic when I learned how to write it, the first Arabic number I learned. I was around five years old at the time.

"Maybe 5th-century BCE." Tim corrected.

"How long does she live?"

"Considerably long, in her mid 30's she is halfway through her life."

Something else came to mind then; I had had a very strong aversion to the history of slavery during my stay in Tanzania.

"Did I ever have a lifetime as a slave?"

"No."

"Why then does it hurt my heart so deeply when I just read about the history of slavery in a travel guidebook?"

"It is recognition of injustice."

I wondered where Tim was at this time in my soul's history. "Allow *yourself* to access, at the same period in time, 5th-century BCE, did you have an incarnation? And if so, where would you be?"

"Nothing came up," Tim responded. But then Tim, who does not believe in afterlife, said something that did not sound like Tim at all. "I have more a sense of being able to watch than being present."

"Like a helper or guide from the spiritual realm? A guardian angel of sorts?" I knew none of these terms would resonate with the atheist Tim and was thoroughly delighted when a trance-bound Tim truthfully responded, instead.

"I feel sort of something like that. Absolutely, like that."

Could this be the explanation I'd been looking for? Was this why Tim could so easily access my past life because he had been my guardian angel?

"So, you are part of it," I commented. "Like when this priestess performs rituals, she is going beyond the physical. What enables her to perform these sacred rites is her connection to a bigger, richer spiritual world beyond the veil. A plane ordinary people have blocked themselves off from accessing easily.

"She is able to open herself up willingly. The oracle-priestess does not have special powers that others do not, she simply has an appetency to remain open, at will, and help others.

"And from the other side of the veil, you are there, a part of it. So, we had a connection back then, too." A feeling of joy filled me upon saying those words.

But Tim had one last, otherworldly, closing remark, "Magical, mystical, close to the gods."

And so, we were.

Epilogue

Halfway through the first draft of *Carol's Lives*, life became remarkably busy with my private practice. For the weeks I was in Vancouver from 2016 to 2018, I worked seven days a week, with many a late night. And when I was not in Vancouver, I was travelling extensively throughout Europe, Africa, China, and Central and South America. In 2017, I stopped writing the book for an entire year. It was not until late May 2018, almost three years after I had started this autobiographical journey, that I decided it was time to finish what I had started.

But my partner Tim and I had to take ourselves out of Vancouver to do it. I always have a hard time saying no to my clients when I am in the city. We ended up in a small village on the Richelieu River in southern Quebec, nestled close to the American border and not far from New York City—a prominent location in the book. For two weeks I wrote furiously in this little haven, so that I might finally finish the first draft of the book.

I do not feel guilty about the delay in completing *Carol's Lives*; everything happens for its own reasons. If I had finished the book earlier, I would not have the current last chapter, *It Doesn't End*. And while I was slowly writing, I felt as though I were combining subsequent editions with the first one; I would discover inspirations for new material to insert into the story to create a more fulsome book.

I realize all past lives are but experiences of the one soul. Experiences are completely subjective, and stories all unfold from these experiences. The past lives are not me; they are not Tim, either; they are the movies, plays or novellas of our souls.

It is always quite confusing for Tim when he comes back from a hypnosis induced trance, like waking up from a vivid dream, it is as if a brilliantly intense world were still going on inside him and here he is, waking up from that time and space reality to this time and space illusion.

Tim tells me that it is similar but more intimate than watching a movie. When you watch a movie, you know you are watching a movie. In a hypnotic regression, however, it is more empathic, you feel as though they are your own feelings, yet from somewhere different. For example, even though they are Carol's feelings, it feels like his own.

Are we able to rewrite the history of our past?

No matter how complex each individual life may be, the thread that is used to weave the patterns is the same. In each of those characters, Carol, Jean, Aarn, Sijo, Saren, and Ramrut, I can find another richness of the tapestry of what makes Tim, Tim—A reluctant patriot, a self-doubting artist, a well-rounded diplomat, an indulgent hedonist, a wandering soul. I genuinely believe by reviewing and learning from these "mind-movies" and feeling the "somewhere different" but "intimate" feelings, we *are* changing the past. Perhaps, healing from and with it.

It is like taking the script of a movie and rewriting it. Or taking a book and adapting it for the big screen.

For myself, I have chosen to designate this lifetime as *the* lifetime of healing and resolution, for the whole of me, so that I may change all the other lifetimes I have lived.

Acknowledgements

To Tim, for being my first unbiased reader of the initial draft of *Carol's Lives*. Yes, writing this book has proven to be very healing. Think about it! Of all the billions of people across the globe, it's amazing how we found our way to each other, our paths converged, and again, life was never the same! I thank you for never doubting my sanity—even when I would not let my mind off the hook in trying to explain something completely beyond its realm.

To my editor Melanie Christian, for your dedication, precision, and attention to details. I could not have asked for a better editor for this book. I felt from day one, you understood me, and this book. You took what I wanted to express and helped me express it so well.

To my nephew Devin Yu, for your willingness in saying yes to my requests. You have helped me hugely, especially at the beginning of my journey as a hypnotherapist. We are so different on so many levels, but no doubt family.

To Orlea Rollins, for the obvious!

To Lucca Hallex, for inspiring me to organize psychic reading circles for Orlea Rollins.

To Jay and Morgan Khan, for your generosity and kindness. Your support has shaped many of the pages of *Carol's Lives*.

To Korë Jackson, for our years of friendship and our connection on an intellectual, emotional, and spiritual level.

To Guy Levesque, for your constant support, positive outlook, and encouragement; from day one of my hypnotherapy career and throughout the book writing process.

To Damien Kiely, for your amazing gift. You walked into my office on the last day of August 2019, seeking answers to your own life's questions. You wished to follow your dreams, and you allowed me to witness your own incredible transformation. I am so glad that you agreed to share your natural gift, by granting me a reading focusing on the parts of Rick Miller that Carol never knew. You enriched the pages of *Carol's Lives* because of it. Thank you for stepping into this with me.

To my clients, for your encouragement and the interest in your eyes when you heard about *Carol's Lives*. Some of you had been hearing the now old news, that I was writing a new book for likely too many months and years. Thank you for your patience.

www.ingramcontent.com/pod-product-compliance
Lightning Source LLC
Chambersburg PA
CBHW020905080526
44589CB00011B/445